PRAISE FOR
THE CRISIS BOOK

"A very comprehensive book for almost any human stress event. Readers will be able to find useful strategies and life tips to improve a stressful situation. Brilliant, practical and extremely helpful."
Dr Patrick Williams, Veteran Life and Wellness Coach, Author & Global Speaker & Trainer. Founder, Coaching the Global Village

"A comprehensive, expert, clear and practical text from authors with unrivalled experience, a valuable addition to any reference collection!"
Steve Boorman, Director Employee Health Empactis, Lead Reviewer National Health Service Staff Health & Well-Being Review

"Well-being and work are closely related. Organizations are now realizing that individual well-being translates into corporate success. This book brings together a variety of aspects that are essential to health and well-being. A must-have for individuals as well as organisations."
Gladeana McMahon, Chair Emeritus, Association for Coaching UK and Executive Training Consultant, Foundation for Recovery and Well-Being Coaching

"A first class 'gift' of a book that a line manager or coach could give to their team or client for them to refer to when faced with a challenging situation. Easy to pick up and navigate, practical and with a vein of empathy that runs strongly all the way through."
Dr Shaun Davis, Global Director of Safety, Health, Wellbeing & Sustainability, Royal Mail Group

Published by
LID Publishing Ltd
One Adam Street
London
WC2N 6LE
United Kingdom

31 West 34th Street, Suite 8004,
New York, NY 10001, US

info@lidpublishing.com
www.lidpublishing.com

A member of:

www.businesspublishersroundtable.com

© Rick Hughes, Andrew Kinder & Cary Cooper, 2017
© LID Publishing Ltd, 2017

Printed in the Czech Republic by Finidr

ISBN: 978-1-910649-31-2

Cover and page design: Caroline Li
Illustrations: Sara Taheri

THE
CRISIS
BOOK

OVERCOMING & SURVIVING WORK-LIFE CHALLENGES

RICK HUGHES, ANDREW KINDER & CARY COOPER

LONDON
MADRID
MEXICO CITY

NEW YORK
BARCELONA
MONTERREY
SHANGHAI

BOGOTA
BUENOS AIRES
SAN FRANCISCO

FOR OTHER TITLES
IN THE SERIES...

CONCISE ADVICE LAB

SMALL BOOKS: BIG IDEAS

CLEVER CONTENT, DYNAMIC IDEAS, PRACTICAL
SOLUTIONS AND ENGAGING VISUALS –
A CATALYST TO INSPIRE NEW WAYS OF THINKING
AND PROBLEM-SOLVING IN A COMPLEX WORLD

conciseadvicelab.com

CONTENTS

PART 2: WORK-LIFE SKILLS

PART 3: MOODS AND EMOTIONS

ACKNOWLEDGEMENTS

This book is dedicated to the hundreds of organizations and thousands of clients the authors have had the pleasure of working with over many years.

It is through them that we have learned to better understand the many issues that cause stress, distress and crisis, but above all how the human being has a huge capacity to change, adapt and recover through determination, resolve and commitment.

Special thanks to Martin Liu, Sara Taheri and all the team at LID for their support, encouragement and professionalism and to Caroline and Tony Redman, Tim and Sue O'Rouke, and Sadia Nujhat.

Rick: To Kirsty.

Andrew: To Jane, Hannah, Isabel and Lydia.

Cary: To Jai, Isabella, Emme, Skyla, Bodhi and Amabel – my wonderful grandchildren.

PREFACE

The popular myth that the word "crisis" in Chinese is composed of two symbols – one meaning "danger" and the other "opportunity" – may well have been most memorably spread by Senator John F. Kennedy during his speech on 12 April 1959 in Indianapolis, Indiana, US. Kennedy was partly right and partly wrong. A correct understanding of a crisis is key to extracting the true value from this important and meaningful book. So pay attention and read deeply to extract the best from what is being offered.

A crisis is in fact a time of danger, a critical moment in time, a time to be wary and alert. A crisis may create fear, but it need not do so. A crisis should get your attention, make you alert, open your mind and enable you to prepare for the right response at a critical moment in time. One of the risks in a crisis is that our emotions take over and our cognitive (thinking) processes shut down. This comes with our genetic history and the stress response that is hard-wired within all women and men. When we rely on these dominant, well-learned responses in a crisis, we may be right and come out fine. Or we may be wrong and make the crisis even worse. Which path is the better path through the crisis?

The authors of *The Crisis Book* have the deep, rich experience and authorative knowledge to offer some wonderful nuggets of wisdom for a wide range of crises that challenge us in our work and our personal lives. No lectures here, no dense reading. However, they have provided wonderful structure and key dimensions of the crisis for you to read and then think about *before* you act. Remember, your thinking shuts down in a crisis. So the authors are thinking for you and with you so that you do in fact make the right moves and take the right path through the crisis. You can first survive and then you can overcome each and every crisis that life throws in your pathway. No need to stumble over these crises, but rather treat them like hurdles that you can clear with skill, effort and with the new ideas, information and wise words offered in this book.

Remember, living life is not rocket science that can be executed with precision engineering. No. Life is messy and complicated, but based on the human science wisdom of the authors, life can be lived with passion and excitement. Crises *are* challenges, and challenges are what enable us to grow, become stronger, live better and feel richer in experience and stamina.

So when you know you are in a crisis, do not panic or become frightened. No ... reach for this good book, begin to read, slow your emotions down and fill your thinking up with the information herein. Once you do that, you will most likely know your right path through the crisis ... one step at a time. A crisis is not the time to get in a hurry, and a crisis is a terrible thing to waste. Take your time, pay attention to the lessons the authors and the crises have to offer, and grow stronger as we know you will.

James Campbell Quick, PhD
Former member, Society of Air Force Clinical Psychologists, Arlington, Texas, US
Distinguished University Professor
John and Judy Goolsby – Jacqualyn A. Fouse Endowed Chair
The University of Texas at Arlington, US and The University of Manchester, UK

INTRODUCTION

WHAT IS THIS BOOK ABOUT?

We start life in this big world and it takes years and years to learn how to grow and develop. We're babies, then toddlers, little young people, then teenagers, youths ... and then we're adults ... for the next 50 years or so!

But things happen in life. Sometimes beautiful, happy and fun times. But also sad, painful and distressing times. In some ways, if we do not experience the bad things in life, then we'd have no capacity to balance this and experience the good times.

The Crisis Book aims to guide you through the many tricky and difficult experiences most of us will go through some time in our lives. It'll help insulate and prepare you before they happen or support you when they do.

HOW SHOULD I READ THIS BOOK?

You choose! We've developed a style so that each chapter provides precise tips and major learning points for you to turn into actions. It means you can dip in and out of the book when it suits you. Many chapters provide further pointers to related chapters.

We hope you enjoy this book and that it helps provide you with guidance and support for many years to come. Above all, we want this to enable you to embrace life and enjoy it more!

Rick, Andrew and Cary

PART ONE

WORK
STRESSORS

1. WORKLOAD

> *"Overwork tires; underwork wearies."*
> (Francis Balfour-Browne, Entomologist)

Work gives us meaning and a sense of purpose and achievement. It gets us up in the morning and provides structure and routine. It helps to define who we are and the work persona that transcends from this. But we can also lose ourselves in our jobs and become work slaves, especially in a long-hours culture.

We form a "psychological contract" at work; a mutual relationship between us, the worker, and the organization. In exchange for the work we do, or outputs, we are rewarded with remuneration and benefits, or inputs. In theory, that's all it takes ... but in reality the demands placed on us can be wholly disproportionate to our capacity to manage them.

Understaffing, business imperatives and tight deadlines all contribute to feeling overwhelmed. An equally distressing contrast exists when we are underworked, overqualified or our jobs lack the demands that we need to motivate us. Both being overwhelmed and underworked require affirmative action.

OVERWORK

SCHEDULE. Prioritize the difficult tasks first; these can be better managed when you have your peak energy.

DELEGATE. Don't hang on to every task; know what to delegate and when. Learn to trust and believe in others. (See Delegation)

PERFECTIONIST. No one is expected to be perfect. Appreciate when it's better to complete all tasks well, against completing only some tasks brilliantly, and vice versa. (See Time Management)

COMMUNICATE. Explain to your boss the pressures you face. Sometimes talking about it to colleagues can help identify solutions.

DUTY OF CARE. All organizations have a Duty of Care toward their staff to reduce the potential for unhealthy stress. You have a right to raise issues about any unhealthy stress that work demands on you.

OBLIGATION. If you feel obligated to take on more and more work, ask yourself why you have this obligation and what benefit this serves you.

CHOICE. You'll feel overloaded if you sense you have no choice. Act decisively where you can and if you genuinely have no choice about the workload, choose how to respond to it.

CONTROL. Strive to bring some control over what you do and the demands on you. Even bite-size feelings of control help illustrate that you have a choice.

STRESS. Know how, why and when you feel stressed ... then act. (See Stress)

UNDERWORK

BOREDOM. Apathy or monotony can be stressful as well. Build in mini-challenges or tasks within your routine.

EXTERNAL. In your non-work life, seek out other ways to express yourself creatively. This may become sufficient to balance any boredom at work.

OPPORTUNITIES. Spot opportunities that haven't been identified by your organization that you could attend to. Can you help someone who's overworked? Can you offer to take on more responsibility somewhere else?

FINALLY
EXIT. If the job doesn't give you what you need, maybe it's not the right place for you. Start searching for a new job.

HEALTH. Give yourself the best tools to cope by attending to diet, exercise, sleep and rest.

HELP. Ask for support. Don't suffer in silence. It's unlikely you're the only one feeling the way you do.

2. CONTROL

"Incredible change happens in your life when you decide to take control of what you do have power over, instead of craving control over what you don't."
(Steve Maraboli, Behavioral Scientist)

Life is often about trying to bring some control into a world of chaos, both at home and at work. There's an unpredictability about everything we do, yet we seem to yearn constantly to exert some control. This causes imbalance, and with imbalance we experience frustration, anxiety, fear and stress.

Often, it's not that we actually need control, but the perception that we do. As if once we regain control, all will be well.

CHOICE. Once you find choice, you find options. How can you be more receptive to options?

DECISION-MAKING. Control, or lack of it, is often caused by a lack of decision-making. If you need more information before you can make a decision, seek it out, then act.

SELF. You might not be able to influence things beyond you, but you can control how you think, feel and behave toward it.

SOLUTION-FOCUSED. If you woke up tomorrow and suddenly had the control you seek, what would be different? In the past, when you had to tackle a challenging situation, what did you discover about yourself?

BEHAVIOR. Do something that you can control, such as exercising, relaxing or meditating. By reintroducing actual control in one area, you may find the need to control reduces elsewhere.

ACCEPTANCE. Appreciate that some things you can't control. No amount of fighting will change it. Take a deep breath and let it go.

FLEXIBILITY. Prioritization and scheduling may help you to determine what's important, what to focus on and what to delay or delegate elsewhere. (See Planning and Prioritizing)

AUTHORITY. As a parent or boss, you'll need to provide some leadership, structure and guidance, which can involve making tough decisions. Take back control by taking action.

CONSEQUENCES. Embrace control and act decisively, rather than worrying about the consequences of making a particular decision. Indecision and denial inhibits taking responsibility.

OPPORTUNITY. Turn hopelessness into hopefulness. For instance, if you're facing redundancy, rather than seeing this as an end, regard it as a potential new beginning, the first day of the rest of your life, an opportunity to reinvent yourself, to reappraise your values and try something new. (See Redundancy)

TRANSFORMATION. Release yourself from the anchors of control by learning to enjoy how *not* needing control gives you freedom, fulfilment and flexibility. This comes with practice and commitment.

MINDFULNESS. Accept, embrace and stay with the "here and now" rather than getting caught up with the past or the future.

3. TARGETS AND DEADLINES

"I love deadlines. I like the whooshing sound they make as they go by."
(Douglas Adams, Author)

Read any job description and you may shudder at the list of "essential" and "desirable" requirements of the job. You're not expected to do *all* these things *all* the time! But you will be oscillating from one task to another, managing competing demands and juggling a series of needs. With your workload will come deadlines; you'll need to complete a task to a certain standard by a specific time.

Sometimes this will create considerable conflict; you'll feel you don't have enough time, there's just too much to do. You'll become anxious, irritated or frustrated at being in this position, and you'll stress out.

Targets and deadlines simply exist to get things done. They're not supposed to be there to judge or persecute you, even if it feels like they are.

INSPIRATION. Consider targets and deadlines as a way to inspire or motivate you, to show what you can do. It's often the fear that's worse than actually getting on with the job.

FLOW. Think of a time when you got so lost in a task that you became totally absorbed. This is getting into a "flow" state, when your focus takes over any emotional insecurities.

PAST. How you dealt with deadlines in the past is not necessarily a reflection of how you'll respond today or in the future. Stay in the "here and now".

CLARITY. Ensure you know what is precisely required and within what timeframe. Without this you have no structure.

MEASUREMENT. A task can be determined by a starting point and an end point. You need to know where each is before you can fill in the middle bit.

FEASIBLE. Make sure you can achieve what's required. If a demand is beyond your capabilities or the timeframe allowed, highlight this to those involved at the earliest opportunity.

DELEGATE. In some cases, you may find you can't do everything yourself. Identify how the workload can be shared and delegate accordingly, monitoring progress as appropriate.

BITE-SIZE. Sometimes doing smaller tasks, one at a time, can be easier than doing everything at once.

NEGOTIATE. If you know you'll struggle to meet a deadline, negotiate a more favorable extension or seek out some leverage on what you'll deliver. It's easier to do this in advance rather than retrospectively.

POSITIVE. If you start a task with "I can't", then you've already opened the door to failure. Get the facts, identify and reach out for the resources, muster what you need and begin with "I can".

SUPPORT. If you don't have the skills or resources required, ask for them. Your organization has a duty to ensure you're provided with sufficient tools to complete a task.

4. BULLYING

"No one can make you feel inferior without your consent."
(Eleanor Roosevelt, US First Lady and Politician)

Bullying happens at any age (from school to work), irrespective of gender (women are increasingly bullied by other women), with no bearing on seniority (senior executives get bullied too), popularity, length of service at work or time at school, or our ability to get on with people.

Bullying can be covert, such as being excluded from groups, work, decisions or information, or more overt, including public put-downs, being embarrassed in front of others or name-calling, insults, physical assaults and shouting.

We're just as likely to witness bullying behavior towards other people. But do we ignore it, perhaps thankful it's not happening to us, or do we take a stand and do something about it? It's not easy.

Usually doing something can be easier than we think. And the momentum of taking action can be very empowering, helping to regain our self-confidence and self-worth.

BE SAFE. First and foremost, however you choose to respond to a bully, violence is not an option. And be mindful of any real threats to your own physical safety.
LEAVE THE SITUATION. If you end the phone call, leave the room or walk away from the bully, then you gain some control and

demonstrate to the bully they have lost power over you.

BE STRONG. You can rise above bullying by believing and trusting in yourself. You know you're "better" than the bully. And the bully probably already knows that too.

REPORT IT. If you report what's happening, the bully may need to account for their actions.

RISE ABOVE. The bully will often have their own problems; maybe they are being bullied themselves. By pitying them, you gain more control, better empathize with their mixed-up behaviors and channel your angst. One way of rising above the bully is to visualize them trying to take off a tight wet suit!

CHANGE. You might not be able to change how the bully acts, thinks or behaves, but you can change how you react and feel about what they're doing.

WIDEN PERSPECTIVE. While you might become obsessive and paranoid about being bullied, it's unlikely to be happening everywhere all the time. Enjoy where and when you are bully-free.

SUPPORT. It might help to speak with a friend or work colleague for support. Maybe they can help you counteract the bullying or stick up for you.

THERAPY. Therapy can help you assess the options you have to manage the effects of the bullying.

KEEP CALM. Often it's how you react to the bully that ignites the fuel for further bullying. But you can stay calm, assert yourself, believe in your self-worth, change or leave the situation and end it.

NAME IT. No one likes to be called a bully. Often the bully doesn't realize that what they're doing is bullying. In the right circumstances, maybe you can tell them that what they're doing is bullying behavior and how it affects you. Often this is enough to end it.

RIGHTS. You have a right *not* to be bullied. (See Assertiveness)

MEDIATION. An independent mediator might help. (See Managing Conflict)

5. WORKING HOURS

"Never get so busy making a living that you forget to make a life."
(Anon)

If we get paid a set fee or salary for a specific number of hours, working beyond them means we're effectively working extra for free. If we're able to confine our work to the hours set, then we do what we can within that time slot. If the work isn't completed, we continue with it the next day.

But in some jobs, a condition of employment can implicitly determine that we need to put in "what the organization requires", meaning we sign up to work more hours than we are remunerated for. It might be a 40-hour-a-week contract, but perhaps we find ourselves working 50, 60 or more hours.

This is a grey area; employment rights in legislation can and do protect us from overwork and organizations have a Duty of Care to provide a safe and healthy working environment, but ... and it's a big *but* ... there's often tacit encouragement or implicit invitation to give more of ourselves.

A "long hours" culture normalizes excessive hours and can lead to sleep problems, poor concentration and, perhaps ironically, lower productivity. It can impact our relationships, family and home lives.

CONTRACT. Check your employment contract for terms relating to hours of work, plus any additional terms associated with "extra requirements". Is there a remuneration payoff for this, can you re-cover time back in lieu of extra pay, or is this what is expected given the job you do?

NEEDS. How many hours do you need to do your job? Do you need to work more efficiently or are the demands unreasonable and unrealistic?

TASKS. Rather than focusing on time generically, consider how you allocate time for each task and how this fits into your schedule.

ANALYSE. Monitor the time you actually work each week against "down-time", including travel, commuting, lunch, coffee breaks, "water-cooler" chats and other informal processes. Are you using your time wisely?

BREAK. Without suggesting you work more for less, ensure that you give yourself sufficient breaks. Recharging your batteries gives you more energy, perspective and capacity.

MODEL. If you're a boss, demonstrate the importance of a work-life balance in how you work.

NON-WORK. Give yourself regular set times for relationships, family and friends. Be strict about trading this for impromptu work demands.

SWITCH OFF. Do something that allows you to switch off from work, during breaks or at home. Creative engagement nourishes the brain, whereas TV can saturate or suffocate it.

PRODUCTIVE. How can you work more in less time? How can you be a smart worker?

WORKAHOLIC. Are you one of them? Re-read the quotation at the start of this chapter and consider how you can bring balance back into your life. (See Work-Life Balance)

REST. To give the time to work, you need to give the time to rest.

6. DIFFICULT BOSS OR COLLEAGUES

> *"Speak when you are angry and you'll make the best speech you'll forever regret."*
> (Laurence Peter, Educator)

We're thrown into a microcosm of work with a diverse cross section of people and cultures, personalities and characters, all weaving their way through the labyrinth of life at work. However, when problems occur and relationships break down, it can feel very frightening, destabilizing and threatening.

A "difficult" boss or colleague usually becomes such because of a breakdown in our relationship. Something inappropriate has been said or done, we may feel wronged or have a sense of injustice, or there's just some wider personality clash. We need to repair the damage and find a way back to a more positive and fruitful relationship.

EMAILS. Avoid firing off an angry or "flame" email, and worse, copying others on it, even if you believe it's warranted. This can aggravate a situation and make matters worse. Emails rarely resolve a situation.
FACTS. Write down the facts, including what's been said or done and when, plus whether there have been any witnesses.
EMOTIONS. Appreciate that there may be strong emotions

surrounding the issue. You might not be able to control other people's emotions, but you can manage your own.

NEEDS. Look at the underlying needs in both yourself and the other person, as this can be the basis for identifying common ground.

FACE TO FACE. Preferably speak with the person face to face, perhaps with a trusted colleague, who will not add fuel to the fire.

PERSPECTIVES. Understand that you and the person may have different perspectives. Assess the differences and similarities to determine potential reasons behind the difficulties.

PRIVACY. Arrange a meeting with the person in a private place where your conversations are not heard by others. This ensures you derive the privacy you both deserve.

RESPECT. Treat the other person in the same way you'd like to be treated yourself. You may have legitimate grounds for your disagreement, but that doesn't mean you should compound things.

OTHERS. Avoid talking to other colleagues about your situation, where people would be encouraged to take sides or escalate the issue, though do speak to your boss or Human Resources.

POLICIES. It usually helps to confront the other person individually and as soon as is practicably possible, but check any procedures your organization has on this subject.

ESCALATION. Your boss has a responsibility to and for you. Consider involving them at an appropriate stage if the issue is about a colleague. If your boss is the problem, assess whether a different boss is more appropriate.

MEDIATION. In some cases, independent mediation is available to resolve conflict. Check with your Human Resources Department.

GRIEVANCE. If you have been unable to resolve the issue yourself, consider formalizing your issue in the form of a formal grievance.

SUPPORT. Consider what support interventions are available, either through employee counselling or through trusted intermediaries.

7. MANAGING CONFLICT

> *"Ten per cent of conflict is due to difference of opinion.*
> *Ninety per cent is due to wrong tone of voice."*
> (Ritu Ghatourey, Author)

Conflict is a people issue, involving a disagreement of some sort between individuals or teams. We all have different needs and wants, aspirations and motivations, objectives and ambitions. There is some inevitability that conflict will occur at times, as we battle our respective agendas. The causes of conflict are often associated with insufficient people skills (management or communication), poor work environments (inadequate training, skill sets or work opportunities) or can be due to harassment or bullying.

Conflicts are a sign of passion, meaning and belief, which is positive. That's normal. But it's how you interpret, deal with and respond to differing views that have the potential to generate a negative conflict.

PRIVACY. Have a quiet word with the person(s) involved in a private setting. You don't want to do anything in a public environment that compounds any negative sentiments. Certainly avoid email! (See Email Etiquette)

LISTEN. Conflicts can emerge because people don't feel heard. If you spend time listening to those involved, you'll also build a better picture of what's going on.

ACKNOWLEDGE. People need you to understand them or appreciate their situation. Whether you agree with them or not, reflect back how you hear their story or version of events.

FEEDBACK. How you say something can have more weight than *what* you say. (See Constructive Criticism)

AUTHORITY. How you portray your authority is crucial to the resolution potential. Are you treating the people involved as "adults" or in a more "parent-child" manner?

RESPECT. Treat the situation and those involved with respect and your decision will be more likely to be respected.

MODEL. You need to lead by example so others can learn from your actions or behavior.

REMOVAL. If tempers are being lost, de-escalate the situation by taking people (and yourself) out of the situation; take a break or walk around the block.

CONSEQUENCES. Your job may require you to stamp your authority and act decisively, but what you do may have consequences for all those involved. Determine if a short-term solution might have longer-term negative consequences. Play to the long game.

FORMULATE. In a state of anxiety, it can be difficult to get the right words out. Plan and formulate your argument with reasoning, substance and correct information, even if this means practising with a script or a trusted colleague or friend.

EMOTIONS. Understand your emotional repertoire so you use the appropriate emotions. (See Managing Emotions)

PROTOCOLS. Your organization may have procedures that can or should be followed in certain circumstances involving conflict. Know what these are so you know when you need to adhere to them. Not only will this protect your position, but they're likely to offer you some "best practice" action.

ASSERTIVENESS. Understand when and how you need to assert yourself and avoid the temptation to act aggressively. (See Assertiveness)

ACCEPTANCE. In some cases, you may simply have a passionate dislike for someone. You might not be able to change them, but you can change how you think, feel or behave toward them.

AVOID GAMES. Beware of falling into tit-for-tat, game-playing behavior. This usually results in a lose-lose situation.

MEDIATION. In some cases, you may need external mediation. This offers an independent and impartial process for conflict resolution. It is often highly successful, as it enables you to have a meeting with a trained professional who will not take sides and will encourage all parties to focus on reaching an agreement or settlement.

8. DIFFICULT CUSTOMERS

"The customer's perspective is your reality."
(Kate Zabriskie, Trainer and Coach)

The service that we provide for our customers is not so much what we do, but how we do it and the relationships we forge. Every type of organization has customers in some shape or form, including the "internal" customers "served" by others along the process chain.

Much of the time, a stable, fluid and equitable relationship ensues; a customer gets what they want and concludes their service acquisition as expected. But sometimes things go wrong, their expectations may exceed what they actually receive, they may come across as hostile, intimidating or aggressive, or they may be determined to get what they regard to be recompense. Some of this may be justified, some of it might not be, but we have to deal with it, either way.

LISTEN. At the heart of any customer response is their need to feel heard. Reflect, rephrase and reconstitute what it is you believe they are saying – this helps to demonstrate you have listened and are keen to find their point of contention.

PROFESSIONALISM. You are your organization's representative and are responsible for defending the company's reputation.

STAY CALM. The customer may be pushing every one of your buttons, but if you lose your temper or lose control, you've lost the situation. Game over.

SPACE. Let your customer speak. Don't talk over them or interrupt; this can fuel further angst.

RAPPORT. Focus on creating a bond or relationship. Make it professional yet personal.

EMPATHY. Actively listen to what your customer is saying and to their unspoken cues and hints.

NON-JUDGMENTAL. Suspend any personal opinion about the customer. You may not get to hear about why they've had a bad day; their car accident, their family chaos at home, their bereavement, etc. These can all inadvertently feed into why they're disgruntled and want things to be better.

COLLUSION. Refrain from reinforcing the customer's angst about your organization, especially if you regard their issue as extremely legitimate and you wholeheartedly agree with them!

FACTS. Stick to the facts, but also recognize that emotions may be swamping the issue. Spot the customer's emotional cues and language; these will allow you some leverage in how you soften the emotionality of the situation. (Emotional Intelligence)

OPPORTUNITY. By resisting a defensive response, you regard the customer's issues as an opportunity for the organization to learn something it might not otherwise have known. If more than one customer has a similar point, then maybe the organization needs to make some legitimate change.

BALANCE. A difficult customer can impact your self-confidence. Recognize and reinforce in yourself the tasks you have excelled in, problems positively resolved and successes achieved.

PROCESS. Take control of the situation by explaining what you can and intend to do next. This may involve suggesting a compromise or offering to "elevate" their concern to a higher authority.

DUTY OF CARE. Your organization has a Duty of Care to provide you with a safe and healthy work environment. It's in both your interests for you to have the tools, resources and training to manage difficult customers.

SUPPORT. It's rarely about you. Don't take it personally. Monitor how this affects you and seek out and use appropriate support.

9. JOB SATISFACTION

"The only way to be truly satisfied is to do what you believe is great work." (Steve Jobs, Cofounder, Apple Inc.)

No job can give us 100% job satisfaction. Most of us at some stage in our work lives will be dissatisfied with our jobs for any of a number of reasons: job insecurity, poor work relationships, mistrust and disrespect, workplace stressors, insufficient remuneration, lack of promotion or opportunity, bullying and harassment, insufficient opportunity to learn and develop, lack of control, responsibility or authority ... and many more.

NAIL IT. Work out *why* you think you are not satisfied in your job. Is it the job or is it something linked to issues at home or how you feel generally?

CONTROL. You might not control your job, but you can control how you act, feel or behave.

EMOTIONS. If you're frustrated, hurt or angry, what's behind these emotions? Learn to be more emotionally intelligent so your emotions help you to find reason and substance. (See Emotional Intelligence)

STRESS. There may be stressors that are clearly feeding your job dissatisfaction. (See Stress)

DUTY OF CARE. Your organization has a duty to ensure you have a safe and healthy working environment. If there is a failure to provide this, you have a right to draw this to the attention of the appropriate personnel.

ACHIEVEMENTS. Reinforce your successes. Make a list at the end of each day of the successes you have achieved, however small they may be.

TALK IS CHEAP. Know when it's appropriate to talk to others and when it's not. Resist fanning the flames of wider dissatisfaction or colluding with any dysfunctional organizational dynamics. Talk about it because you want a resolution, and talk only to those who can influence this. (See Politically Astute)

POSITIVE. Act positively and you reinforce positivity. It can be easy to moan about your job. Act negatively and you reinforce negativity.

NETWORK. Build professional networks in your organization and beyond. Engaging with others may allow you to see your job differently, or may connect you with people who can offer you the better opportunities you seek.

HELP OTHERS. Take the focus away from you and your job and help someone else in theirs. This can give you a different perspective on yours.

WORK-LIFE BALANCE. Get a life beyond work and you'll see your job as only part of your wider world. (See Work-Life Balance)

SUPPORT. Don't suffer in silence. Seek available support where you can; a trusted colleague, your manager, Human Resources or a therapist.

GET OUT. In some cases, maybe you're not meant to be doing the job you have and there's no alternative. Life's short enough without wasting years swimming in a pit of work-triggered depression, angst and dread. But ...

CAUTION. It's easy to be lured by the fantasy of chucking in your job or plotting how you'd like to resign to your boss – act in haste, repent at leisure. *And* be respectful and professional if you do decide that leaving your job is the right thing for you. You'll be amazed how frequently in the future you'll bump into the people you used to work with!

10. DELEGATION

"You can do anything, but you can't do everything."
(David Allen, Productivity Consultant)

Successful delegation is at the heart of effective teamwork. The struggle emerges in learning how to "let go", use your own time resourcefully, and encourage and inspire others to contribute to the greater objective. Many problems associated with work overload emerge from a failure to delegate. We may be perfectionists or want full credit for a task. Or we might consider that others lack the sufficient skills to take on a task. This can be loaded with irrational judgments, such as, "They won't do as good a job as me," so the delegation block remains. Maybe they won't do the *same* job as you, but what if they can? What if they can do a better job than you? Is it not worth a try?

CONSEQUENCES. What are the consequences of delegating or *not* delegating and are these real or imagined?

INVESTMENT. Delegation can be "front-loaded" in that you may need to put the time in first, but this can be a short-term time investment for a long-term team-development and outcome benefit.

RESOURCES. Reassure yourself that the person you delegate to has the resources needed, including the time and skills. Part of your responsibility is equipping them with these.

LEADERSHIP. Delegation is not only about how you can develop others, but it's a skill that can define your ability to trust, inspire, encourage and motivate – all key leadership skills.

DEFINE. Be clear exactly what the task is and whether this is suitable and appropriate for delegating.

CLARITY. Problems occur when a delegated task lacks precision and explicitness, giving grounds for ambiguity. Keep it simple and explain the purpose, value, meaning and objective, plus, if appropriate, a potential pathway to achieving the preferred outcome.

MEASUREMENT. Know what the start and end points are. Some tasks can be left to your team member to consider how they get from "A to B"; others may need more guidance and structure.

TRUST. Most people want to do a great job if they're trusted to get on with it. The more you trust, the more likely this trust will be returned, respected and rewarded.

COACHING. Keep in touch before, during and afterwards with open, non-judgmental communication. Encourage questioning and clarification. Adopt an informal style.

CONFIDENCE. Some people balk at being given responsibility and lack the self-confidence, despite having the necessary skills. How can you instil and inspire confidence in that person?

SUITABILITY. Some tasks are more suited for delegation than others. It's your call. Major decisions may involve more serious or critical issues.

CONSULTATION. Don't be afraid to "scout" for further feedback before deciding to delegate. Perhaps you need more input, information or insight to allow you to do so.

TRAINING. Can your fears associated with delegation be tempered by specific guidance, advice or skills training?

AUTHORITY. Delegate authority, not responsibility, as you are still accountable to how, what, why and when you delegate, plus the outcome.

LEARNING. As you learn to delegate and others take it, offer constructive feedback, as appropriate, to applaud success, review insights and highlight learning opportunities or needs.

11. NOT KNOWING

> *"Being at ease with not knowing, is crucial for answers to come to you."* (Eckhart Tolle, Author)

We have an insatiable appetite for knowledge, yet sometimes knowing can be a burden that locks us into a predefined construct. Our past life experiences can shape how we "need to know" and can be negatively influenced by friends, parents and teachers. Educational systems place great emphasis on the acquisition of knowledge rather than the pursuit of thinking, learning and "being".

We fear the outcome or consequence of not having enough knowledge, skills or training and so can consume ourselves by a swamp of information. No one knows everything. It's impossible. The ideal scenario is "knowing enough" and seeing "not knowing" as a blessing rather than a curse, an opportunity rather than a hindrance and as healthy rather than an ailment.

CURIOSITY. Allow yourself the opportunity to be inquisitive, to ask questions and to inquire. The more outlandish your curiosity, the wider the perspective you'll generate.

MISTAKES. Learning from mistakes can be our greatest developmental asset. Normalize, accept and appreciate the potential of mistakes to turn this into a mine of opportunity.

CREATIVITY. Painting by numbers never reveals an artist's voice, so how can you tap into your creativity to find your own picture?

BOUNDARIES. Structure comes from certainty, yet it limits the world within this structure. How can you "step out of the box"? How can you be a "disruptive" thinker?

CHOICE. Not knowing often invites the opportunity for choices. Seek them out, appraise and select them to give you options you might not otherwise entertain.

PHILOSOPHICAL. In a work world where you may be constantly asked "what is the answer?", twist this around and consider "but what is the question?"

TEAMWORK. Most successful people achieve greatness because they have great people around them. Appreciate others who have what you do not. (See Delegation)

ADVENTURE. The pursuit of real adventure does not lie in having a perfect plan executed with military precision; rather it's about adapting to uncertainty.

CALM. As you juggle demands and deadlines, not knowing can give you space and freedom to "be in the moment" and truly open up yourself to a greater and more real experience.

CELEBRATE. Applaud how you embrace not knowing and how you worked with this or overcame it.

(See also *Not Knowing – The Art of Turning Uncertainty Into Opportunity* by Steve D'Souza and Diana Renner (2014) LID Publishing, London)

12. CAREER DEVELOPMENT

> *"Opportunities don't happen, you create them."*
> (Chris Grosser, Entrepreneur)

We're often so busy doing our jobs that we rarely pause to reflect on where we're going in our careers. Maybe we're happy enough in what we're doing, which is great. However, it's still worth taking stock of our career. Some people reach a plateau, which is enough for them, but by standing still we can be overtaken by other people, events, new technology, processes, systems and change.

Our career can be scripted through our personality and our inherent capabilities, as well as our upbringing, education, initial employment and a hodgepodge of life events contributing to being in the right place at the right time or, in some cases, the wrong place at the wrong time! A job is not for life anymore. We change jobs, our jobs might be made redundant, organizational change might alter what we do, relationship and family demands might impact our jobs, finances may dictate work needs, and our own values and interests will influence what we enjoy or want from work.

VALUES. What do you really enjoy, what gives you satisfaction and inspiration, what gives you meaning? How have your values changed and why?

PRIORITIZE. What's a non-negotiable "red-line" in terms of what's vital and important to you? Is it money, responsibility, authority, leadership, social value, people focus, fun, a social life through work, etc.?

RESPONSIBILITY. You are responsible for the decisions you make at work and this includes towards your choice of job and career. Often, feeling "stuck" is fed by apathy, inertia and not acting to do something different.

PLANNING. Meet with a career advisor to explore how your traits, skills, needs and experience can offer you new career opportunities, including utilizing psychometric tests or undertaking training courses.

INSPIRATION. What or who inspires you and how can this knowledge encourage you to make changes? What would they do or say to you? What type of work inspires you or would get you out of bed in the morning?

INDISPENSABLE. Avoid being indispensable in your job, as you may be regarded as "impossible to replace" and therefore bypassed for more general promotional opportunities.

NETWORKING. Meet lots of people to widen your career landscape. Most new jobs and careers emerge from people you know and the doors they can open for you. Don't forget social media.

MENTOR. Find someone more senior who can help shape, influence or advise you on your career destiny.

AVERSION. What's stopping you from developing further and is this due to any self-confidence or self-worth issue? Talk to a therapist to unravel how you might be colluding with the problem.

NON-WORK. Don't forget your life beyond work. The activities, interests and pursuits you expand your horizons with may open up new opportunities and allow you to meet different people and learn about their work. (See Work-Life Balance)

PRESENT. While it's important to monitor where you are in your career to ensure you remain focused, happy and engaged at work, don't become preoccupied with the pursuit of change or scaling the career ladder ... wake up and smell the coffee; enjoy, savour and celebrate what you have.

13. PROMOTION

"There is no future in any job. The future lies in the person who holds the job." (George W. Crane, Psychologist and Columnist)

Promotion is what we may strive toward in our careers but we can sometimes overlook the potential pitfalls associated with overpromotion or underpromotion. With overpromotion, we may find we are out of our depth, with insufficient skills or experience demanded by the role. This often happens when someone is promoted because of time-served in a specific role, yet is unprepared for the extra responsibilities regarding managing others.

Underpromotion leads to apathy and boredom and can emerge because of a lack of job opportunities or insufficient stimulation. Both overpromotion and underpromotion can lead to stress, anxiety and depression, albeit for different reasons. There's a discrepancy between our capabilities and what the job offers.

TAKE STOCK. Step back and assess where the problems exist and disentangle what's related to the role and what's connected with your abilities. Identity your needs and wants, why they are not being met and what you can do.

FEEDBACK. Ask your boss or a trusted colleague to provide objective assessment of your situation so you can generate an alternative angle; 360-degree feedback can widen your perspective.

SIDEWAYS. Promotional bottlenecks occur when people above you do not vacate their roles. Consider a sideways shift to gain new or extra skills and experience.

CHANGE. The negative consequences of under/over promotion occur when you feel stuck and unable to do anything. Explore opportunities to change what you do or how you do it and this can sometimes open the door to a new perspective.

CONFIDENCE. Your confidence might take a hammering. Reflect on the things you do, or have done, well. Believe in yourself and appreciate that the situation can change.

GROWTH. See any limitations or deficiencies as beacons of growth, development or learning rather than as something that defines you.

TRAINING. Consider what skills you can learn to improve or change your situation. Even non-work skills connected to home life or your hobbies can help develop your skill sets differently.

LISTEN. Hear what your colleagues, manager or family are saying to you. They may be giving you important cues or messages that you have not seen and which are impacting them.

POSITIVITY. It's easy to get sucked into negativity, blaming the organization, your boss or colleagues. Stay focused and positive and you'll become more receptive to the solutions.

HELP. Ask for assistance, support, guidance or help. You don't need to deal with this on your own if other people can give you the key that opens the door.

OPPORTUNIST. Whether underpromoted or overpromoted, dig for the opportunities that will shape where you need to be. Take courses, network, meet people, read, learn and talk. Sometimes you might not see the solution because it's right in front of you.

14. PLANNING AND PRIORITIZING

"The key is not to prioritize what's on your schedule, but to schedule your priorities." (Stephen Covey, Author and Educator)

Pretty much everything we do is a conscious response to planning and prioritizing; we make a decision to do something at a specific point in time. But much of this is also subconscious, as we act "in the flow" of the moment.

As we juggle more and more, at work and at home, we need to develop some kind of plan or else things will slip or we will slip up. People, demands and circumstances will always conspire against us. But applying some principles can help.

URGENT AND IMPORTANT. What's urgent and important, what's not urgent but important, what's urgent but not important and what's neither urgent nor important? For example, the ringing of a phone suggests it's urgent, but it might not be important. It might be more important not to take the call and finish the task at hand. The aim is to work on tasks that are not urgent but important, so with good time management you deal with them before they become urgent. (See Time Management)

CONSEQUENCE. A good way to determine if a task is urgent or important is to consider the consequences of *not* completing it.

VALUE. Typically 80% of your work will represent 20% of the value. Focus on the 80% of the value.

COLLABORATE. If you are uncertain what constitutes a priority task, ask or seek clarity with others.

PHONE BATCH. If you need to make a series of calls in a day, group them into one time slot. This will help you focus on the act of making the calls, rather than jumping back and forth.

PLANNER. Stick up a wall planner calendar for key dates and to give you a visual summary of time.

FIRM. Stand your ground on what *you* determine needs doing, why and when. (See Assertiveness)

CONTROL. Many factors seemingly beyond your control will influence your planning. Factor in these variables to build in some wriggle room.

TIME-STEALERS. Be resolute about resisting time-stealers. These can come in the form of ineffectual meetings, lack of decision-making, reworking tasks that were not planned properly at the start, and unproductive conversations. What are your time-stealers?

LEVERAGE TIME. Be realistic about the time needed for tasks. Rather than squeezing everything in to a tight time frame, give yourself some review, recap and recovery time.

DELEGATE. Share the load, monitor and feedback delegated tasks. (See Delegation)

DEFEAT. Know when to admit defeat. Some things just aren't meant to be completed in the way you'd like and within the time you have.

REVIEW. Always evaluate progress. What can be better next time?

BREAKS. Build in time for breaks and interruptions ... as well as having a bit of fun!

15. ORGANIZATIONAL CHANGE

> *"The secret of change is to focus all of your energy, not on fighting the old, but on building the new."*
>
> (Socrates, Philosopher)

Companies need to move forward, remain productive and seek out better ways of doing things. Unfortunately, this is often achieved by making changes. And many of us don't like change. This affects everyone. With any change comes a prospect for losing something. And it's this fear that drives our anxiety.

Anxiety is an important human emotion, which warns of threats. We may fear changes to our jobs, staffing changes, impacts on authority and even the threat of losing our job. This then triggers added anxiety about how we'll cope with each eventuality and what happens next.

INVOLVEMENT. Get involved in the process as soon as possible, and likewise, involve others if you are an architect of change. People react defensively when change comes out of the blue. Provide consultation groups and feedback forums. Allow for a two-way process; otherwise it can feel like a lecture where decisions have been made irrespective of people's views. Folk feel ignored and de-valued if this happens.

COMMUNICATION. Invite discussion and dialogue. Organizations often limit change decisions to a few key people, but conversation can open the door to new opportunities and ideas that haven't been considered.

INFORMATION. Seek out or share the rationale behind the need for change. If people understand the *why*, they're more likely to accept and engage with it.

MORALE. Appreciate that morale can be affected, including an increase in office politics, corporate in-fighting and gossip. Deal with this promptly by using your skills of empathy to understand the sentiments behind the anxieties and what can be done to manage these better.

ENGAGEMENT. Change needs staff commitment. Scope out potential threats to engagement. It's a normal response for some people to retreat, but you want to inspire and motivate these people to journey in the right direction, through dialogue, insight, sharing and communication.

INDIVIDUALIZE. Group contagion, back-biting or gossip can trigger a strong resistance to change, forming a subculture of antagonism. Speak with people individually and privately to allow them an opportunity to feel involved and for their issues to be heard. Don't do this just for the sake of it; make it real.

DECISIVE. Change needs to be quick, well informed and put in place as soon as is practicably possible; otherwise it can generate a cultural malaise of mistrust, ambiguity and uncertainty.

EXPECTATIONS. With a cloud of anxiety brooding, clarify and formalize expectations of the process, including what people have concerns about. Ground decisions with facts and figures, reason and rationale.

ABUSE. People can "kick out" and react negatively to the prospect, reality or the consequences of change. Similarly, organizations can exploit the workforce when in a position of power-infused change. Be alert to both and explore what you can do to manage this – harassing or bullying others is always unacceptable. (See Bullying)

OPPORTUNITY. Change can bring about positive benefits and outcomes. Motivate and inspire your team to think similarly. Look for the silver lining.

BALANCE. Change at work can feel all-consuming. Ensure you can disengage and retain a life at home too. (See Work-Life Balance)

16. POLITICAL AND ECONOMIC UNCERTAINTY

"Peace. It does not mean to be in a place where there is no noise, trouble or hard work. It means to be in the midst of those things and still be calm in your heart." (Anon)

We will experience, endure and grow through one crisis after another. And there's no exception in the wider political and economic environment. In democratic societies, the public has the power to vote a government in or out. Organizations expand or retrench and industries blossom or decline.

We're all part of a global political and economic system and so we experience the highs and lows accordingly. It can generate huge anxiety and uncertainty, especially when we live our lives reliant on the order and structure of a stable government and a flourishing economy.

KEEP CALM. It might not seem so at the time, but things usually get better. You might not be able to change the situation, but you can take responsibility for how you feel or react. It can take time to regroup, but most problems can be overcome.

OPENNESS. Don't be afraid to vocalize how this impacts you. Openness attracts support from others and gives permission to voice the struggle with uncertainty.

DIALOGUE. Talk about what's going on with those affected. They may have a different perspective and could offer a solution or a positive way forward.

REALITY CHECK. Check you have the correct facts and clarify the exact reality of the situation.

FOCUS. Concentrate on what you can do, not what you can't. Focus on one thing at a time.

TIME. Things might not resolve overnight. Accept that you may have to allow time for a resolution.

TRANSFORMATION. Search for the opportunities for growth and development, both personal and professional.

ACCEPTANCE. Stop the stress meter by pausing and accept that you are where you are.

PREPARATION. As part of learning, assess how best to plan for the future in a changed environment.

WHAT MATTERS. Consider what's really important here. Are you still alive, do you still have a roof above your head?

PERFECTION. Striving to be perfect fixates into static positions. It's OK to make mistakes as you find the way to sail through unchartered waters.

KNOWING. You can't know everything. Not knowing gives you the chance to learn, to know. (See Not Knowing)

TOLERATE AMBIGUITY. Go with the flow. Can this give you leverage over some of the new opportunities?

INSTINCT. Trust your instinct, both in terms of what to do now, and also in preparing for the future.

CONTROL. You can't control everything, but you may be able to control the immediate impact on you or how you feel or respond to your situation.

GOALS. Ensure goals are realistic and achievable. You need to savour goal fulfilment.

CONTINGENCY. What have you learned about the current situation that can give you the tools, resources or hindsight to prepare for the future?

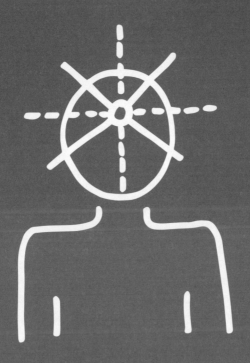

PART TWO

WORK-LIFE SKILLS

17. TIME MANAGEMENT

"The best way to get something done ... is to begin."
(Anon)

At the heart of time management is the concept of prioritization. We have to prioritize over a series of tasks to determine how we schedule what we do. It's about what's important to us and, if we do not complete an action, the cost or consequence to us.

We devise a strategy based on information about the task. We understand that we need to know what the task is, any potential deadline, how long might it take, the cost or consequence if we succeed or fail, and how or why we might prioritize. This starts to add up to a lot of decisions. Bingo! Time management is totally impossible without the ability to make decisions. And by not making decisions, we procrastinate.

AIMS AND OBJECTIVES. Ask yourself: where are you starting from and where do you want to get to?
WORK SMARTER, NOT HARDER. It's about the quality of the work you do in the time allocated, not necessarily the amount of time you spend. It might be more productive to give yourself short blocks of time to work, say thirty- or forty-five-minute segments, have a break, then start again.

URGENT AND IMPORTANT. The aim is to clarify here what's urgent and important, what's not urgent but important, what's urgent but not important and what's neither urgent nor important. The aim is to work on tasks that are not urgent but important, so by good time management we deal with them before they become urgent.

DAILY "TO DO" LIST. Plan for the day so you don't get surprises ... but also build in time for surprises!

DEADLINES. Do you need to build in a "false" deadline to kick yourself into gear? Do you find that you leave work until seconds before the deadline or do you plan to meet a deadline with some buffer time left over?

COMMITMENT. Determine how long each task might take and what is required of you.

EARLY FINISH. If you aim to make the deadline with seconds to spare, think of the stress you put yourself under. It's better to build in some buffer time or leeway.

SAY "NO" OR DELEGATE. To be effective, decide what's reasonable and possible. If you're asked to do something that's unreasonable and impossible, can you say "no" or can it be delegated to someone else?

HAVE A BREAK. You need to recharge your batteries to give yourself energy to complete all the tasks in your schedule. Have a break that's actually restful, calming and relaxing.

MANAGE EMAILS. Much of your days will be spent dealing with emails. Be smart about how you manage your emails, so they work for you, not against you. (See Email Etiquette)

EXPECTATIONS. Manage the expectations of others, especially those who may waste your time. Be assertive about what you are able to work on. (See Assertiveness)

18. RESILIENCE

> *"What lies behind us and what lies before us are tiny matters compared to what lies within us."*
> (Oliver Wendell Holmes, Poet, Physician and Author)

Resilience is about being able to cope with tough situations and bounce back from difficult experiences. It can help us better deal with traumatic events or times of considerable stress. It doesn't mean we'll never face problems again or that we'll be immune to life events. It just means we'll be better protected, better prepared and better equipped to deal with them.

Better to spend a small amount of time understanding how to be resilient, rather than endure the emotional cost to us of not doing so. You never know when you might need it.

PURPOSE. Having a firm sense of personal beliefs, values and intent gives you the power to progress through tough times with conviction and resolve.

PEOPLE. Forge positive relationships with family and friends. Reach out to bolster your wider community through networking meetings, social media and family events. Having a rich pool of contacts and connections offers leverage and sources of help in a range of situations.

GROUPS. Engage with community organizations, faith-based communities and voluntary associations to widen your sphere of influence and avail yourself of social or spiritual sources of help.

HELP OTHERS. Assisting others provides a feel-good factor and bolsters positive self-worth and well-being. It will also reinforce in you the value of, and acceptability of, asking for help when required.

PERSPECTIVE. Introduce a reality check so you don't interpret problems as being worse than they are.

GROWTH. Regard stressful events as opportunities for growth and transformation. (See Life Cycle Losses)

ACCEPTANCE. Appreciate that bad things do happen and plans can change. Seek out a new reality and focus on the new opportunities and options that invite a better way forward. Seeing a therapist might help achieve this perspective. (See Therapy)

REALISM. If you find a trend forming in tough situations that is affecting you, take a step back and reassess how you can protect yourself or shift to a more realistic game plan. Are you attracting adversity?

CONFIDENCE. Trusting and believing in yourself can give you the positive self-esteem to combat adversity. (See Developing Confidence)

BABY STEPS. Rather than trying to solve world peace overnight, focus on bite-size achievements, one at a time.

SELF-CARE. Know what you need to relax, look after yourself, and give yourself physical or psychological nourishment.

REFLECTION. After events, assess how you coped with the situations and how you might deal with them differently in the future.

HELP. Don't be a martyr. Find ways to ask for help and know who to ask. (See Asking For Help)

19. ASSERTIVENESS

"Assertiveness is your ability to act in harmony with your self-esteem without hurting others." (Anon)

How we choose to communicate with the world around us determines how assertive we are. It's not about shouting the loudest or talking over other people (though sometimes we might have to!). It's about being heard. We've all met someone who has a quiet voice, yet is the person to whom people listen most. So it's not about the volume, but the content and delivery of what we say and the confidence by which we express what we say.

Therapists frequently use the concept of the "Assertiveness Bill of Rights" to affirm the positive nature of assertiveness. It's a series of personal statements, which we can learn to apply to our lives to boost our self-worth, self-esteem and our ability to be more appropriately assertive.

1. I have the right to ask for what I want and need.
2. I have the right to choose how to lead my life in a way that suits me, rather than others.
3. I have the right to say "no" to requests or demands that are unreasonable.
4. I have the right to express my thoughts and feelings, whether positive or negative.
5. I have the right to change my mind for my own reasons.
6. I have the right to make mistakes and learn from them.

7. I have the right not to have to be perfect.
8. I have the right to develop and follow my own values, beliefs and standards.
9. I have the right to say "no" to anything that threatens my values, beliefs and standards.
10. I have the right to determine my own objectives, goals and priorities.
11. I have the right not to be responsible for others' behavior, actions, feelings or problems.
12. I have the right to expect honesty, dignity and respect from others.
13. I have the right to be angry and to say, "I'm angry."
14. I have the right to express different emotions to reflect how I feel.
15. I have the right to feel scared and say, "I'm afraid."
16. I have the right to not know and to say, "I don't know."
17. I have the right not to give excuses or reasons for my behavior or reactions.
18. I have the right to make decisions based on what I believe to be correct.
19. I have the right to focus on and fulfil my own needs.
20. I have the right to personal space and my own time.
21. I have the right to be playful and have fun.
22. I have the right to be healthy, wealthy and wise.
23. I have the right to be in a non-abusive or threatening environment.
24. I have the right to make my own friends and enjoy their company.
25. I have the right to change, develop, learn and grow.
26. I have the right to have my needs and wants respected by others.
27. I have the right to be happy and enjoy life.
28. I have the right to supportive, nurturing and positive relationships.
29. I have the right to ask for help.
30. I have the right to be *me*.

(Adapted from *The Anxiety and Phobia Workbook* by Edmund Bourne, PhD, New Harbinger Publications, Oakland CA. 6th Edition 2015)

20. CONSTRUCTIVE CRITICISM

"Criticism, like rain, should be gentle enough to nourish a person's growth without destroying their roots." (Frank A. Clark, US Politician)

We need to be free, willing and able to learn by making mistakes, and any constructive criticism needs to offer motivation, inspiration and encouragement. Persistent destructive criticism can damage self-confidence and self-worth. It's all about how we give feedback to others, and how others provide feedback to us.

GIVING FEEDBACK

FEEDBACK SANDWICH. First give some positive context or praise, then highlight the issue that needs improvement, and finish with a compliment or something else positive.

KEEP IT BRIEF. Only refer to a minimal number of criticism points; otherwise a long list of critical points will sound like you're bombarding them and they'll either switch off or dig their heels in.

BE SPECIFIC. Be clear about what specific point you are making; otherwise it might get lost in your waffling.

BEHAVIORS. It's crucial to focus on a specific behavior that has been observed rather than giving a personal opinion. It's not personal and so shouldn't be made to feel as such.

DON'T ASSUME. It can sometimes feel personal if you make wrong assumptions about the person you're criticizing. For example, if someone's late handing in a report, don't assume they're lazy or couldn't be bothered. They may have a good reason.

TIME AND PLACE. No one likes being embarrassed in front of others, so be mindful about appropriate privacy and timing.

OWN IT. It helps to contextualize criticism within your own experiences, so try something like, "This is something I always got wrong but then I learned ..." so you can normalize the issue.

OPEN AND HONEST. Being transparent helps to maintain trust, integrity and honesty.

PAD IT. If time allows, soften what you're saying at the start of the conversation, rather than diving straight in. Help the person engage with you so they can hear what you're saying.

FACTS. People hear facts, but can get caught up and confused if a message is layered with your own emotion, anxiety or stress.

OPTIONS. If you're giving criticism, offer some ideas or options that the person can take to remedy the situation; otherwise they may remain stuck with what to do next.

BE POSITIVE. Stay positive and model how the criticism is a "positive learning opportunity".

FOLLOW UP. If you've given criticism, be available to support the actions that you recommend to remedy the situation.

RECEIVING FEEDBACK
POOR SKILLS. The person giving you feedback might be inexperienced at giving constructive feedback. Show them this book!

NOT PERSONAL. Much of what you hear can be negatively selective if you're anxious and mistrustful.

LEARNING. Embrace constructive criticism as a learning opportunity.

CLARIFICATION. Sometimes we react negatively to criticism if we don't understand it or we feel misunderstood. Therefore, reflect and clarify what's being said so both sides understand better.

21. EXAM PRESSURE

"Trust yourself, you know more than you think you do."
(Benjamin Spock, Pediatrician and Author)

Examinations are tests that demonstrate our ability to learn or confirm what we know about a subject. In adulthood, after many years of not being tested, we might find ourselves needing to boost our knowledge and take a dreaded test. Much of the dread is associated with fear and anxiety.

What suits one person may be different for someone else. We just need to find what works for us, but preparation is likely to be important.

LEARNING STYLE. Do you revise better early in the morning or late at night? Does it help to read aloud or highlight text on what you're revising, or maybe write it down, record it and play it back? Writing revision cards or spider diagrams can be helpful, especially if you are a visual learner.
COLLABORATION. Does it help to work with a friend who's also studying the same subject? Maybe you can test or ask each other questions to help pick up any gaps in your knowledge.
EAT. If you're anxious, you may lose your appetite, but as the brain needs feeding, you need to eat healthily. Limit high-fat, high-sugar and high-caffeinated products, especially for children, as this may increase moodiness and hyperactivity, and reduce concentration.

HYDRATE. Drink lots of water, as headaches can result from not being sufficiently hydrated.

SLEEP. Feeling rested, calm and awake helps you learn and concentrate, so you require the normal amount of sleep that you need, waking and retiring at the time that suits your working style.

KEEP CALM. Before and during exams you might feel panic. This can be managed by regulating your breathing, taking long deep breaths and exhaling slowly.

EXERCISE. It might seem that you won't have any time for exercise when you're studying, but it can help to stimulate your body, increase oxygen and blood flow and help rejuvenate you.

COMPUTERS. If studying on the computer, or if "relaxing" with social media or computer games, switch these off at least an hour before bed, so your body can calm down and relax for a good night's sleep.

BREAK. We tend to learn best in chunks of 45 minutes, so build in breaks.

ANXIETY. We all experience some degree of anxiety. You can only do your best. Your worst fear is unlikely to happen and even if it did you would survive and work through it.

DON'T COMPARE. Especially when you're taking exams with friends or colleagues, there can be a lot of people bragging about how much they know. And after taking the exams, the dreaded post-mortem conversations can make you feel that everyone did better than you. Resist the pre- and post-exam chat.

SCHEDULE. To give you the best chance, plan out the time you need to learn what's required. It's really about taking your own responsibility for this. Very few people in this world get by without studying, learning and working, despite what others might say! We all have to.

22. DEALING WITH REJECTION

"Often, you think when you are rejected that you are not good enough, but the truth is they weren't ready for all you have to offer."
(Melchor Lim, Writer)

Rejection is the refusal to accept, use, believe, acknowledge, to throw out, discard or rebuff. To reject something requires us to form an opinion or judgment. We're making a choice that we don't want something. And there may be a very logical reason why we're making that judgment. But when it involves people, people have feelings. And our feelings can be hurt.

How we determine our response to rejection can be heavily influenced by our upbringing, social and cultural context, together with the value, importance and priority we place on the success or the achievement. We are social creatures who want to belong and be accepted. To be faced with rejection is counter to this instinct.

EMBRACE DIVERSITY. Thankfully, we're all different. That means some of us are naturally going to be better at some things than others. And you can't argue against that. It's a fact.
REALITY CHECK. Sometimes we have a misguided assessment of our chances of success. Retreat, take a step back, brush yourself down, re-evaluate, focus on the next stage, concentrate, apply and proceed.

SOCIALISE. Much rejection is directed by others and can have the feeling of a social rejection. It can help to do something positive to engage socially – join a club, go to a social function, engage, communicate and have fun with other people.

EXERCISE. You can feel flat, lethargic and low in energy when you suffer a rejection. Going for a walk helps, as does running, dancing, going to the gym, swimming and pretty much any other physical activity. (See Exercise)

DROP THE PAST. Rejection can feel worse when you automatically link it to a previous rejection or a similar trauma in the past. In this way, you fail to let go of the past and it just continues to haunt you. In this context, if the past is often being triggered, therapy can help to untangle issues.

DEPERSONALIZE. Recognize that a rejection is not personal. You just didn't fit what they wanted. Actors get it all the time; but going to auditions is a necessary part of breaking through.

SPREAD THE LOAD. What about applying for more than one job, asking several different people out, entering several competitions? If you always have "another" chance, it can mitigate rejection, as you balance a rejection with the hope of success elsewhere.

SELF-CARE. Don't deny that rejection hurts. Instead, accept it's happened, that it makes you feel lousy temporarily, and you deserve a little bit of pampering or fun.

SELF-APPROVAL. The only approval you really need is from yourself. Self-respect, self-worth, self-confidence and self-belief can help. Try to see setbacks as development opportunities!

23. DEVELOPING PURPOSE

"The purpose of life is not to be happy. It is to be useful, to be honorable, to be compassionate, to have it make some difference that you have lived and lived well."
(Ralph Waldo Emerson, Poet and Essayist)

As we grow and develop, our purpose may change. Life presents us with strong urges to adopt new purposes at each stage. If we get married, we might focus on our relationship. If we raise a family, the children might take centre stage. Or our purpose may come from our career or a new job.

Developing purpose is about finding a meaning, principle, reason, belief, enjoyment and/or motivation. When things come together to generate passion, this passion then enables us to further grow and develop physically, emotionally, spiritually and/or psychologically.

LEARN. With learning comes wisdom. And wisdom gives you more choices. To learn, you need to apply yourself, focus and spend the time and effort required. Nothing comes in life from nothing.

TAKE RESPONSIBILITY. Only you are ultimately responsible for you. But you have to account for your actions. Taking responsibility means taking ownership of life by learning from your mistakes and making positive changes.

BE INQUISITIVE. Learn about purpose by asking questions. No one knows all the answers, but there's always someone who has an answer. By asking, you learn and understand.

INSPIRATION. Who inspires and motives you and why? What is it about them that has this effect on you? Might you be an inspiration and motivation for others?

NEEDS AND WANTS. Understand the differences. Needs are often basic and necessary for survival and normal functioning. Wants are the optional extras. What constitutes a need or want in your life?

LISTEN TO YOURSELF. Often you get so lost in the stimulation around you that you don't hear your inner voice, what your body, mind and soul are telling you.

LISTEN TO OTHERS. Active listening is a learned skill, whereby you don't just listen to words spoken, but to the wider area of body language and non-verbal cues.

ENGAGE. Humans are social creatures and so you need to communicate, engage and interact with others. This can be at work and at play where you seek an equal role and voice.

CONTENTMENT. Being content conveys a settled acceptance of happiness, where you're not driven to hedonistic ecstasy but one that embraces joy, peace, calmness, relaxation, spirituality and tranquillity.

UNDERSTAND BELIEF. What do you believe in, why is it important and what purpose does it serve? Is it religion and spirituality, sports and recreation, or even work, achievement or making a difference? Don't shun these aspects of yourself, as they may contain a hidden answer to your life's question.

LEGACY. Imagine you're on your deathbed at the age of 100. What would you say to yourself? What regrets might the 100-year-old have? The challenge is to come back to today and ensure that these regrets do not happen!

24. CONFIDENCE

"Who looks outside, dreams;
who looks inside, awakes."
(Carl Jung, Psychiatrist and Psychotherapist)

Confidence is a very personal affair with oneself and often influenced by how we feel others think of us. But most people are far too preoccupied with themselves to have the time or inclination to think about us!

Negative opinions about ourselves often come from the past: a critical parent, ineffective teacher, judgmental friend or dominant partner. These people, and others, can cloud the reality of how we regard ourselves. Confidence is about developing a positive self-worth, appreciating the uniqueness, individuality and the value we bring to our world. It's believing in our abilities and having an assurance or trust in ourselves.

KNOW THYSELF. Who are you? Know your thoughts and feelings. What are your beliefs, passions and values? What's important to you and why?

BE POSITIVE. Self-defeating thoughts feed insecurity and self-doubt. Think positively by taking action with an optimistic intent and a determination that things can improve.

PASSION. What you believe in gives you energy and commitment. Develop passions for things that give you meaning, value and purpose.

PREPAREDNESS. If confidence comes from doing a task well, then plan what is required to do the task well. Prepare the groundwork to give yourself the tools you need.

LEARN. Having knowledge, skills and competencies gives you the skills and ability to act confidently.

ACTION. Indecision and uncertainty emerges from not prioritizing what you need to do; improve your time management and organization. (See Time Management)

POSTURE. You can actually feel confident by how you hold yourself. Pay attention to "walking tall" and holding your posture, rather than slouching, and feel the difference this makes. Try this exercise: stand and imagine you are an oak tree with roots coming out from your feet into the ground – this gives a sense of strength, groundedness and confidence.

STRENGTHS. Play to your strengths rather than being preoccupied by your weaknesses.

ARTICULATE. People will listen to you better if you speak with considered pace, clarity and assertiveness. Pause for effect.

APPLAUSE. Give yourself a pat on the back and the credit you deserve for the things you do well.

FORGIVENESS. Give yourself permission to make mistakes and forgive yourself for errors.

WORRY. If concerns and anxieties are sapping your self-confidence, identify the causes and do something to eradicate them or learn how to manage them better. Seeing a therapist might help.

DRESS. How you dress can affect your self-confidence. What effect do different colors have on your image and how you feel?

SMILE. What makes you smile? Do more of it. The more you smile (and that's smiling naturally!), the more you make other people feel better and you raise your own-self-esteem.

25. WORKING WITHIN A MATRIX CULTURE

"Culture eats strategy for breakfast."
(Peter Drucker, Management Consultant and Author)

Organizations have traditionally operated within a hierarchical structure, i.e., from the top down. Increasingly, this is shifting to one defined as "matrix". which is much flatter and operates over a series of interconnected departments, divisions and teams. "Matrix management" engages managers across a wider set of roles and responsibilities, often with more than one team, product or service at any time. Everything becomes more interchangeable and inter-related while providing the potential to adapt to changing priorities.

It increases fluidity and flexibility, and it reduces the silo mentality of specific people or departments strictly sticking to their domain. It involves more people, so offers greater problem-solving and a dexterity of thinking, and it encourages personal engagement and empowerment. But it can present significant challenges: roles can be complex and difficult to define, which impacts responsibility and authority. It also presents potential conflict between working styles.

REMOTE. If you work off-site or from home, invest time in developing your work relationships and networks and make the most of opportunities for on-site visits to forge these face-to-face connections. (See Remote Working)

OBJECTIVES. Be clear of the expectations within your role, so you understand what you are being measured against, particularly regarding appraisal points.

DEMANDS. Conflict can arise where there are competing priorities. Learn how to negotiate with your stakeholders so that priorities can be appreciated in the wider picture of organizational outcomes.

CLARIFY. Seek clarification from team or departmental heads about prioritization. What you regard as at the top of the list might not be the same for your superiors. Don't assume you know; the remote and flexible nature of a matrix culture breeds ambiguity.

RESPONSIBILITY. Understand deadlines and targets, plus your role in seeking to meet them, especially when juggling priorities, which might be a constant facet of multitasking.

COMMUNICATION. Establish an appropriate communication mechanism, so you know when best to meet, speak on the phone, email or instant message, as a means to share progress or request input.

MENTOR. Seek out someone who can guide you through the matrix jungle and connect you to and through the appropriate channels.

TRUST. Tasks can form and develop with new unknown team-members, which can present trust issues. Establish norms by which clear communication and control of objectives feed into a mutual need and achievement of trust.

SOCIAL. Utilize social opportunities with staff as a way to develop work relationships and manage more informal information sharing and "soft" networks.

OPPORTUNITIES. Embrace the diversity and dexterity that a matrix culture offers. Learn from the different working styles to develop new ways of managing your workload and executing your tasks.

26. SOCIAL MEDIA

"The dark side of social media is that, within seconds, anything can be blown out of proportion and taken out of context."
(Nicola Formichetti, Creative and Fashion Director)

Social media has transformed how we work, and the world has become an open window to our lives as huge amounts of information float in, out and through a heap of networks and online platforms. Organizations promote their products and use these resources as powerful advertising and public relations mediums. It's also used for recruitment and a means to define a corporate culture.

But think how much time we waste on it, too! Whether it's checking up on what our friends are doing, reading up on the latest car launch or posting funny videos involving cute animals, the lure of the non-work side of social media can be hugely enticing.

Many crises have occurred as a result of inappropriate use of social media. Like many people before you, you could lose your job over it.

POLICIES. Read your company policy regarding the use of social media. This will present guidelines pertinent to your workplace.
BOUNDARY. Define your own boundary between what constitutes "work" social media and what is "non-work" and understand how and when each can be accessed.
DISCLAIMERS. Beware the temptation to spout forth under an

apparent disclaimer of "these are my personal views". They might well be, but you are still an employee of your organization. People inadvertently merge personal and work personalities together.

RESPECT. Treat others as you would like to be treated.

ALCOHOL. Guard against posting anything while under the influence of alcohol. It might sound amusing to you after a couple glasses of wine, but may take on a very different perspective the morning after.

PERMANENCE. There are ways to delete posted material, but some social media do have terms and conditions that give them copyright and a right to maintain your material "in perpetua", i.e., forever.

JOB IMPACT. At some time in the future, you may seek a promotion or a new job. Recruiters read social media. What do your postings say about you? Your boozy trip with your pals might make hilarious reading to your friends, but would your employer share the same sentiments?

POLITICS AND SPORTS. We probably all have our personal political views, but shouting about them online has the potential to alienate some people who don't share your views. In a similar vein, slamming the Chelsea football team might go down well with your Manchester United friends, but your Chelsea-supporting CEO might not agree.

CONSEQUENCES. Think before you post. What impact might your post have?

CONFIDENTIALITY. In work-related social media, be aware that you may be privy to privileged, confidential and commercially sensitive information. If in doubt, leave it out.

SECURITY. Accessing social media on a work computer may involve accessing open platforms that can be at risk of malware and viruses. Ensure you have appropriate information technology protection installed and in operation and social media access is permitted.

HARNESS THE POWER. There are new social media systems that are secure and established solely for a work group. Some employees may prefer to use these rather than old-fashioned emails.

27. EMAIL ETIQUETTE

> "For email, the old postcard rule applies.
> Nobody else is supposed to read your postcards,
> but you'd be a fool if you wrote anything private on one."
> (Judith Martin, Journalist and Author)

Email etiquette is concerned with creating an appropriate environment, and communicating what we say and mean in the tone and manner that will present an accurate picture of our intention. A lot of the time we might not think first; we fire something off and suddenly someone feels insulted or hurt and we have to spend time placating and apologizing. The failing of email is that it's one-way. It doesn't allow for the ebb and flow of human interaction.

EMOTIONS. Resist zapping off an email when you're angry, emotional, drunk or all three. Prepare a draft, if you have to, but sleep on it or leave it for 24 hours before sending it, if at all.

CAPITALS. Avoid using capital letters throughout your email. This reads as if you are shouting.

CC. This stands for "carbon copy" and is what you use to "copy in" others beyond the main recipient. Consider why you need to "cc" someone. It can be perceived as you covering yourself or trying to make a point to several people.

BCC. The "B" means "blind", where addresses are not revealed. Use this to conceal the email identity of those in a multiple-addressee email, especially to protect the privacy of those who might not want other people to see who they are or their email address. Using blind copies can be seen as devious; why would you want to hide names?

STYLE. We all have different email styles and language skills. When starting a new job, explain your email "manner", how and why you email the way you do, this will avoid misinterpretations.

VOICE. Consider when it is better to speak to someone by phone or face-to-face. There are many situations when email is much less appropriate, particularly when discussing sensitive issues.

REDUCE. Emails can be a waste of your time and in the organizational context, managers should be encouraged to speak with their teams rather than to hide behind their computer screens.

FORMALITY. Some emails can be simple, with no salutation or sign off, especially to work colleagues. Others may require greater formality and courtesy depending on the context and recipient.

THINK. Consider how you say what you say and the consequences of anything you send. Could it be misinterpreted? Think before you send. Once it's sent, it's sent.

RESPECT. Treat others as you would want to be treated.

PREVIOUS. Start a new email for each message; otherwise you will have a long stream of emails that may be difficult to follow. Though, in some cases this may be an important record of activity and views.

CONFIDENTIALITY. Know your organization's email policy, particularly regarding confidentiality and how to communicate externally.

'D'EMAIL. Delete the emails that are unimportant; **D**elegate or forward emails for others to take action on; **D**efer emails you need to consider further; **D**o respond when required; **D**rop it into an appropriate folder and be aware which emails are purely **D**istracting; like the holiday offer or shopping deal. (See Time Management)

28. LEARNING FROM MISTAKES

"Your past mistakes are meant to guide you, not define you." (Anon)

In most cases, we make a mistake because of our choices, perhaps because of inadequate information and/or a misguided intention behind the choice. We either make a mistake innocently (we believed we *had* made the correct choice) or we do so knowing it to be an error.

Most of us would argue we make mistakes because we are ill-informed or ill-advised and do so honestly and without intent. But we often think "we should have known better" and this feeds the frustration behind having made a mistake.

LEARNING. We don't like to make mistakes, but it's human nature. We need to remember that we learn from them, and often painfully so.
ADMISSION. The start of learning is to first admit you have made a mistake. Denial simply locks you into a frozen state of inaction, even if it's a self-protective mechanism.
TAKE RESPONSIBILITY. Put your hands up and say, "I have made a mistake, it is my responsibility." It takes courage to own up, confidence to stand firm, and commitment to do something about it. If you have impacted someone else, be determined to put things right.

SEVERITY. How important or impactful was your mistake? Was it an unthinking, silly error (you left the milk out of the refrigerator) or more significant (you committed a crime)? The consequence determines the severity.

CONSEQUENCES. A decisive response may help to shore up the impact. What new intelligence can you muster to "right" any "wrong"?

AVOIDABLE. Could you have avoided the mistake? Why? This is part of the learning process.

REASONING. Understand how and why you made the decision. In hindsight, perhaps with new and better-informed information, would you have made a different choice? If yes, then perhaps there is some appreciation that you acted in good faith.

SAVING FACE. You deserve respect and appreciation for the courage it takes to own up to your mistakes.

PERMISSION. We learn from mistakes, even if it is painful. But in order to learn and move on, you need to give yourself permission to be able to make a mistake.

PREVENTION. What can you do to ensure this mistake doesn't happen again?

TOUGH DECISIONS. Sometimes you'll have to make tough decisions, where you have no clear, positive options, and where you might be cornered either way.

DON'T TRY. You might say, "I'll try not to do that again." But the "try" suggests a lack of effort or commitment. Repeat your conviction without using the word "try"!

EMOTIONS. You might not be able to change the mistake or the consequence, but you can change how you feel about it. Accept it has happened, move on and learn. Don't beat yourself up continuously.

BETTER. Appreciate the personal and unique opportunity the mistake has given you to learn, develop and improve. Lucky you!

29. POLITICALLY ASTUTE

"People with good intentions make promises, but people with good character keep them." (Anon)

Being "politically astute" is having the intuition to appreciate that competition and rivalry exists throughout organizational life and that we can all fall inadvertently into corporate power battles, strategic games and brinkmanship.

Departmentally, this can involve the internal battle for resources and, individually, it might be about jostling for promotion. It can be about individuals who manipulate their personal agenda for some self-serving interest.

OBSERVE. Watch and listen, especially to non-verbal cues. Read the full situation. Spot the early signs of power battles and office politics.
CONFIDENCE. Believing in yourself is halfway to projecting self-confidence to others. You need to be able to demonstrate your successes and achievements, and this means subtly letting others know.
INTUITION. Develop tact and diplomacy. What you say to one person might be interpreted differently by another. You need to understand these implicit differences in people. (See Empathy)
GUARD. Moderate how you project yourself. You want to keep some mystique and allure about yourself. This makes you interesting. But

it's finding a balance between this and projecting self-confidence and assuredness.

ALLEGIANCES. Some people will want you "on their side" for office power battles. Be cautious about committing yourself, as you'll get pulled into their battles. You can empathize how this is important, but ask to remain neutral or play for time and say you want to think about things.

TOUGHNESS. If you are aware there are office games going on, sometimes you're a part of them whether you like them or not. Don't exacerbate or fuel an already volatile situation. Your job could depend on how you act. Be factual and objective rather than making personal accusations.

LOYALTY. Loyalty is synonymous with trust and yet if it's at the expense of someone else, then it has consequences. If you have two bosses gunning for the top job and they both want your support over the other, be aware that if you make a choice, the one you don't choose might get the job.

PROMOTION. In your own career development, you want to position yourself to increase promotional opportunities. This might mean connecting and engaging with those who can influence this. This doesn't make you a "political player"; it makes you someone who wants to learn and develop.

PLEASER. You'll probably spot the person who tries to do everything possible to please their boss, particularly at the expense of you or others. Don't let this dishearten you, but be confident in your own set of values and behavior.

BOSS. A clause to the "pleaser" point above is to recognize that your boss will have more power than you, and will be able to do and influence things in a way that you will not. It's about learning to appreciate and respect this, and knowing where it can help you, but not at the expense of others.

RADAR. Keep your head down and get on with your job. By all means use your "political" radar to become mindful of the office games that get played, but resist getting involved. Your radar is an important early warning alert beacon. Use it wisely.

TRANSPARENCY. Being an open, real and honest broker will help you resist getting pulled into organizational politics, but be careful that you don't reveal your hand too early.

IMPRESSION. Just as you can learn to read the situation by what others say and do, people will be watching you too. Focus on how you want to be regarded: honest, trusting, dependable, committed, open, non-political, averse to mind games and self-serving agendas.

30. REMOTE AND HOME WORKING

> "We like to give people the freedom to work where they want ... whether they (are) at their desk or in their kitchen. Yours truly has never worked out of an office, and never will."
> (Richard Branson, Entrepreneur and Founder of Virgin Group)

Flexible working arrangements are opening up, increasing opportunities to work from home. It might seem like an incredibly tempting luxury with your home comforts nestled around you and the end of the drudgery of the daily commute, but it can be tough to get it right. It requires discipline, commitment and dedication. It can be lonely and isolating. And the temptation to do the housework or DIY jobs can be enticing. However, you can become more of your own boss.

EXPECTATIONS. Clarify what is expected of you, when, where and how. You won't have anyone physically there, but you'll still have demands and deadlines.

STRUCTURE. Identify your goals, objectives, priorities and schedule, just as you would in the office, and keep to them.

COMMITMENT. It takes dedication to get into a workable routine. Plan, practice and stick to it.

WORKSPACE. Choose a suitable working location, with a dedicated desk and office chair. Make it look and feel like an office, organize your desk, place your laptop and phone like you would in the office.

INTERACTION. If you're at home on your own, you might feel isolated. Connect with people when you can; your local daily postal worker may seem like your new best friend!

BOUNDARIES. Focus on developing boundaries between work and home and protect the sanctity of both.

TIME. Develop a routine by starting and ending at set times. Build in breaks and rest points.

DRESS. Donning your slippers and keeping your pyjamas on until midday might sound alluring, but it won't get you into "work mode". Dress sensibly to inspire you to work.

MEETINGS. Get to each face-to-face meeting you can, both with work colleagues and stakeholders. This will help you build face-to-face connections that you may lack when you're working at home.

SOCIAL MEDIA. Resist personal social media by avoiding the temptation to check your apps every hour.

HEALTHY. Keep fit and healthy; get out when you can and build in an exercise plan. Eat at regular times and guard against snacks ... just because no one's watching doesn't mean you should do it!

PARTNER. If you have a partner who lives with you, discuss the pros and cons of this with them, so they understand when you're talking incessantly because they're the first human you've seen all day!

COMMUTE. You might not think you'll miss the commute into work, but this period serves an important function in gearing you up to the start of the day and offering a decompression time at the end. Factor in some comparable activity to give you this time at home.

ENJOY. Embrace the opportunities that home working allows, if you're stuck on a problem and need some mental space, go for a walk. It's your call. Be sensible about the opportunities you have and make it work for you. Don't be too strict with dos and don'ts, but do review with your boss how the remote nature is working for you.

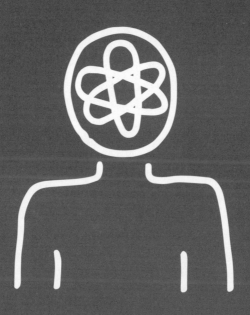

PART THREE

MOODS AND
EMOTIONS

31. EMOTIONAL INTELLIGENCE

"IQ may get you through the door. EQ will determine how far you go."
(Anon)

IQ is regarded as intellectual intelligence (Intellectual Quotient) and EQ refers to emotional intelligence.

Emotional Intelligence is about "being intelligent about emotions". The quotation above reflects the fact that intelligence, as we know it, is based on the qualifications we achieve academically and the intellect this gives us to make cognitive decisions. But we also have a heart that shapes how we connect and communicate with other human beings. Our life will be defined by how well we get on with others and build strong relationships, both at home and at work.

SELF-AWARENESS. Do you understand the nuances of when you're sad, depressed, happy, distraught, elated, lonely, enthused, apathetic and so on? Each conveys a defined emotion in response to a specific set of circumstances or variables. Identify the cause and effect.
SELF-MANAGEMENT. Do you know how and why you manage your emotional feelings and responses at any given time? What is necessary, sufficient, reasonable and appropriate? You decide. (See Managing Emotions)
SOCIAL AWARENESS. Have you grasped how and why others feel

and express emotion? What are their triggers or cues? Do you understand and appreciate where they're coming from? (See Empathy)

ACTIVE LISTENING. Are you really listening to what others are saying, not just the words, but the unspoken messages behind the words? Use all your senses to listen (visual, tonal, body language) and reflect back your understanding of what the other person is saying to clarify and demonstrate that you have heard them.

MOTIVATION. Are you self-motivated and know what drives or inspires you to get on and succeed? What do you need to allow this motivation to lead you? What excites you and why? This creates passion and self-belief in yourself and others.

SORRY. If you make a mistake or say something inappropriate, apologizing is an important conciliatory response that can help to build appreciation, openness, trust and honesty.

NON-JUDGMENTAL. If you stereotype or rush to form your own personal opinion about others, you're making a judgment that can give you a misinformed reality of the person. Be open, transparent and accepting of other people's needs and wants.

INDIVIDUALITY. Get to know the real people you interact with – their loves, their hates, what inspires them, what demotivates them.

FRIENDSHIPS. Who are your real friends and why? They are often people who energize you, give you new perspectives and stimulate your thinking. How can you spend more time with them?

STRESS MANAGEMENT. How you deal with stress affects people around you, at home and work. Know your stress triggers and learn to adapt or manage them better. (See Stress)

TRUST. Trust is a two-way street – trusting yourself and trusting others. You can't learn to trust others if you haven't learned to trust yourself.

CONSEQUENCES. Understand the emotional consequences of your actions. How will people feel about, or emotionally react to, the decisions you make? What are the alternatives?

32. ANXIETY

"Anxiety's like a rocking chair. It gives you something to do, but it doesn't get you very far." (Jodi Picoult, Author)

Anxiety is the brain's response to feelings of threat, challenge or stressful events. But sometimes routine may trigger this physiological adrenalin response, so we feel that we're always in a state of "fight or flight". And with this, we'll regard more things as a threat to us, even if the reality is that they're not. We become anxious, on edge, finely poised to "react". If this is constant, it's exhausting.

Often we may have difficulty concentrating because we're preoccupied by a worry, we're over-exaggerating the real threat to us or putting things out of proportion. It's like things build and build and just spiral out of control. It feels like there's no way out. We can make the anxiety worse by trying to be perfect or trying to control everything.

We all differ in how we show we're anxious. There's often a sense of restlessness, feeling twitchy, having sweaty palms or a flushed face, breathing more quickly, feeling light-headed or having more headaches and migraines. It can feel quite debilitating.

BE POSITIVE. Perhaps you're anxious about a meeting. You can either tell yourself, "I'm going to screw it up" or "I'm going to be great!" Positivity grows by feeding it positivity.

NEGATIVE THINKING. How do self-defeating thoughts help you? They don't. Treat any intrusive negative thoughts as just that – thoughts. Leave the thoughts to one side and act positively. You have a choice.

CATASTROPHIZING. Often, we fear the worst of what can happen. "What if I muddle my words in a presentation?" "What if I *don't* know the answer?" But what if you switch this inner voice: "What if I don't muddle my words?" or "What if I *do* know the answer?"

REALITY CHECK. If you do muddle your words, you're very unlikely to explode or die. That's the reality. If you don't know an answer, would you really get fired? Most likely not.

SELF-CRITICISM. Do you mull over failures and not successes? Is everyone perfect all the time? Even if you feel you didn't handle a situation well in the past, that doesn't mean that this will always be the case.

BE MINDFUL. Anxiety often comes from things from the past or worries about the future. You can't change the past nor can you control the future, so you're stuck in the present! Stay in, and embrace, the here and now.

CONTROL. You can't control what the weather will be like tomorrow. Sometimes it's about enjoying "going with the flow", being open to new experiences and being grateful that no one's perfect.

BEHAVIOR. If you develop an anxiety habit, do something that changes your psychological state: get out of the room, go for a walk, listen to music, find a distraction or breathe in a new perspective.

ALLY. Embrace anxiety as your friendly "threat-detector", offer thanks, and bid farewell; it's done its job.

BE CALM AND CARRY ON. Monitor your breathing:, inhale through your nose slowly, hold for a few moments, and exhale through your mouth slowly. Regulating breathing helps to reduce your heart rate and give you a sense of control and calmness. (See Panic Attacks)

33. DEPRESSION

"It's hard to answer the question 'What's wrong',
when nothing's right." (Anon)

Feeling low or sad is something we all feel at times. It's our body's natural retreating response to certain difficult situations. Normally, this doesn't last long and we'll soon be back to our old selves. Sometimes it can be caused by a chemical imbalance in the brain. There are, however, ways through depression.

IDENTIFY THE CAUSE. Is there an obvious trigger for how you feel? Often, feeling down is a normal response to something sad. Just knowing why you're feeling depressed can help. Perhaps there could be a series of interconnected causes?

EXERCISE. Physical exertion releases endorphins in the brain that can help to improve mood. Exercising with others can provide social contact, which can reduce feelings of isolation and loneliness.

DIET. Having a balanced, healthy diet can make you feel good and improves your sense of well-being. But eating loads of fatty, sweet or salty food forces the body to work much harder and can contribute to an increase in weight, illness, apathy and general sluggishness.

WEIGHT. Being overweight (and underweight) can put a strain on your body. Not only can this make it difficult to maintain a normal level of functioning, but you may become further depressed by associated feelings of low self-confidence and self-worth. (See Weight Management)

WORK. A job (whether paid or not) provides routine and purpose, something to get up for in the morning, a personal identity in the job you do, social contact with others, structure to your life and an income that gives financial security. Work is usually good for you.

ALCOHOL. Many of us drink alcohol to relax. But alcohol's also a depressant. So if you're drinking because you're already depressed, it won't help. It'll not only make you feel more depressed, but it could become something you rely on more, both physically and psychologically. Managing depression can be tough enough without adding an addiction to it. (See Addictions)

DRUGS. There's a link between recreational drug use and depression. Drugs might alter your mood for the short time of the "high", but there will always be some "down" response. What goes up, must come down. The craving can increase in an effort to seek a greater effect. It can lead to addiction.

THERAPY. Sometimes you may not understand why you're depressed or you won't know what to do about it. Talking to a therapist can help to find the source or just to find ways to help you cope better with it. Also, talking to others who share similar struggles can help in letting you know that you're not on your own.

DOCTOR. Your medical doctor is responsible for your health, and that includes your mental health. It's important that they're aware of any depression you might have. They'll also have some options for you and sometimes a combination of medication, counselling and self-help can work well. Avoid sleeping pills, as this can create addiction and rarely deals with the underlying cause of depression.

34. ANGER MANAGEMENT

> *"Do not let the sun go down while you are still angry."*
> (Ephesians 4:26-27, New International Version, Holy Bible)

Anger is a core emotion associated with feelings of threat or danger, a sense of injustice or wrong, or because of frustration or unhappiness. But many of us confuse anger and aggression, which means that our own expression of anger can be inaccurate or misplaced. Anger can be a legitimate means to assert or protect ourselves. If we don't express anger, we may be bottling up an important self-expression and inadvertently contributing to high blood pressure, heart problems, depression, anxiety, colds, flu and digestion issues.

But there's a thin line between a healthy, short-term and appropriate expression of anger and a destructive, brooding, vindictive and potentially violent aggression. Effective anger management is twofold: how we deal with our own anger and how we react to anger from someone else.

ANGER IN OTHERS
FIND THE REASON. What is really going on for them that's triggering their angry outburst? By understanding, and appreciating, how and why other people might express anger, you will learn how to articulate your own anger or your response to theirs.

APPROPRIATE. Even if you do find out why they're angry, is it appropriate? It might be overblown, or a far stronger reaction than is appropriate for the situation. It doesn't mean it's right or that you have to just absorb it. (See Assertiveness)

ANGER IN YOURSELF

COUNT TO 10. Take a time out and count slowly from one to ten, so you can calm down.

SPONTANEOUS. Sometimes, the difficulty with anger is that it's an immediate, unprepared response but ask yourself, "Why am I feeling angry here and why now?" You can think and act differently based on what your answer might be.

BUILD UP. Not all anger is spontaneous; it can be the result of brooding over something or a repeated "drip-drip" build-up effect. Take a step back and consider how to stop this escalation; get out of the situation or change something.

DEEP BREATHS. Take a deep inhalation through your nose and slowly exhale through your mouth. Breathe in and count to four, then breathe out and count to eight. Do this a few times to help calm down.

EXERCISE. A good walk can sometimes help you calm down and put things into perspective. Any form of exercise might help. (See Exercise)

REDUCE STIMULANTS. Some stimulants like coffee, tea, tobacco and alcohol can make your feelings of anger worse. Reduce stimulants to calm down.

IT'S GOOD TO TALK. Talk it through with someone. A therapist can help you work through your reaction and responses. (See Therapy)

MANAGE STRESS. As stress is a key contributor to anger, it's helpful to understand what causes you to feel stressed and what you can do to better manage it. (See Stress)

INWARD. Depression is sometimes caused by "inwardly turned anger", where patterns of blaming or hating yourself start to corrode your sense of self. (See Depression)

35. PANIC ATTACKS

"If fear hasn't killed me yet, then nothing will."
(John Mayer, Singer-Songwriter)

Panic attacks are moments of fear and intense anxiety that grip us for a short period of time, but are relatively common with 5% to 10% of the population experiencing them at some time. The effects can be disturbing and frightening. We feel trapped and get a sense of not being able to escape. We know when it's happening because our bodies start to react.

Because they have such an impact on us, we become hyper-alert to the slightest signs of an attack. Often our body may be reacting to a normal response, perhaps a change in our breathing, or our temperature or our heart rate. That can immediately lead us to misinterpret the signs and push us into the panic attack mode.

MODERATE OR SEVERE. Everyone can suffer from moments of panic associated with shock or fear and that can be a normal reaction. But more sustained and regular attacks may mask more complex triggers, beyond the scope of what you can resolve here – in which case it may be worth seeing your medical doctor or therapist.

SYMPTOM MANAGEMENT. Panic attacks are a mix of physical sensations and how you worry about things. Isolate the thoughts or fears from the physical reactions to bring more choice or control into how you react.

DIARY. Keep a diary of the thoughts, feelings, emotions and actions that take place when you suffer from a panic attack. Build up a picture of what sparks an attack. Reflect on whether you can choose to think differently, act differently or behave differently. A therapist can usually help.

ALCOHOL WITHDRAWAL. Reducing sustained alcohol consumption can cause withdrawal effects and this can feel like anxiety or a mild panic attack. It's prudent to manage any reduction in consultation with your medical doctor.

CAFFEINE. Caffeine is a physical stimulant, which can speed up your heart rate and cause a natural heightened state of alert. It's often what panic attacks feel like in the early stages, so for sufferers it's worth moderating caffeine intake from tea, coffee, fizzy drinks and dark chocolate.

BLOOD SUGAR. A sudden drop in blood sugar can lead to a boost in adrenalin, which can make you feel unsteady, trembling and twitchy. Eat a healthy diet at regular and routine times, and avoid fasting and diets.

MEDICATION WITHDRAWAL. Stopping or reducing a prescribed medication, particularly for depression or anxiety, may set off different moods and feelings as your body adapts. Any reduction in medication should be managed in consultation with your medical doctor.

SMOKING CESSATION. The effects of stopping smoking are usually limited and temporary, particularly the so-called withdrawal "pangs". But they can induce mild feelings of anxiety.

BREATHING. Tackle panic by controlling your breathing. You may be hyperventilating, which causes your heart to beat fast and leads to the intrusive thoughts of having an attack. Learn to breathe slowly; breathe in through your nose, counting to four, and then out through your mouth, counting to eight.

TEMPORARY. They don't last forever. Panic attacks do pass.

36. MANAGING EMOTIONS

"When I say 'manage emotions', I only mean the really distressing, incapacitating emotions. Feeling emotions is what makes life rich. You need your passions." (Daniel Goleman, Author)

Emotions serve the important human function of expression. But sometimes we might feel that the emotions we express are not appropriate or they're out of control.

This chapter focuses specifically on managing emotions, which is the sequel to the chapter on emotional intelligence.

KNOW YOURSELF. You experience emotions many times during each hour of your working day. You don't have an emotion just for the sake of it. You form an emotion in response to something that's happening around you.

EMOTIONAL TEST. Get to know your emotional self with a simple monitoring test. Carry around a notepad and at a set time, say every hour, record what you're feeling (the emotion you're experiencing) and why.

EXPRESSION. Once you know what emotions you're experiencing, you're in a better position to scale the intensity of that emotion. Anger, for instance, can range from mild irritation to being in a blind rage.

CONSEQUENCE. If you react without thinking, you can unleash un-intended consequences. You have the power to manage these con-sequences if you introduce a "consequence awareness meter" into your reaction time. Pause before you attack others. Ask yourself how this is going to solve the situation.

24 HOURS. If you find yourself reeling with an intensely negative emotion, it can be difficult to react objectively. Get out of the situation, change what you're doing or how you're feeling and commit to *not* re-acting for 24 hours. This helps you reintroduce reason and rationality.

NUANCES. Humans have the capacity to detect tiny nuances of emotions in each other. Consider a tiny flick of an eyebrow or a twitch of a smile that can convey so much information. What hidden or implicit cues are you picking up or giving off?

EMPATHY. Once you've better understood your own emotional make-up, you're more able to understand others and empathize with how others are feeling. It works in two ways: the more you understand your-self, the more you understand others, and vice versa. (See Empathy)

JOURNEY. Managing emotions is a life-long journey. You'll be shift-ing, adapting, evolving and learning throughout your life. Writing down your feelings in a journal can help you understand them.

DEEP FREEZE. Emotions are an important part of your makeup, yet many find expressing them so difficult, as though they weaken us or the emotions themselves can overcome and destroy us. Expressing your emotions is actually a strength – take them out of the "deep freeze", so they can help you. (See Therapy)

37. NEGATIVE THINKING

"Once you replace negative thoughts with positive ones, you'll start having positive results."
(Willie Nelson, Singer-Songwriter)

Motor-racing drivers on an oval circuit were found to be "hitting the wall" because they had developed a negative anxiety about doing just that. Subconsciously they were steering into the wall. After confronting this negative thinking, they learned to avoid it.

Our perspectives of the "glass half full" (positive) or the "glass half empty" (negative) peppers how we choose to perceive or interpret the world around us.

When you drive a car in winter, you might worry about ice. That's not negative. That's your brain cautioning you to moderate your speed and drive according to the adverse conditions. But if you worry about ice on the road all the year round, you'd probably see this as pointless. Again, that's negative thinking.

Sometimes you validate your negativity by saying, "If I prepare for the worst possible outcome, then I'm ready for it!" But is the worst always going to happen? Probably not.

BE WITH POSITIVE PEOPLE. There's nothing like being with negative people that breeds your own negativity. Connecting with positive people helps you learn to think and behave similarly.

IDENTIFY THE WORRY. If you can isolate the deep-seated angst, frustration, fear or concern, then you can choose how to combat that emotion before it triggers negative thinking. (See Managing Emotions)

REALITY CHECK. Negative thinking is often void of reality. If you consider the reality of the situation, with the reality of the outcome, you'll often be faced with a different overview.

BODY LANGUAGE. How you hold yourself can affect how you feel. Slouch or stoop and that'll feed into how you feel. If you sit or stand upright, confident, assured and bold, then you'll feel self-assured and positive.

CALM DOWN. When faced with spiralling negative thoughts, *stop!* Give yourself a minute to take stock, breath calmly, relax and give yourself the space to respond.

EMBRACE THE GOOD. Often we get so sucked into thinking about bad, destructive things that we lose sight of the really good things we have going for us. Write a list of what's good in your life, however small, as this can help you see and believe that things are actually quite good in your life.

THOUGHTS CREATE FEELINGS. Replacing negative and self-critical thoughts with more positive self-accepting thoughts starts by accepting that negative thoughts are no longer helpful to you and are creating negative feelings and outcomes.

ACT POSITIVELY. Do something actively positive. Phone a relative who's lonely, help a family friend with gardening, coach a kid on a subject you know something about. Feeling good about what you're doing helps you get into a habit of feeling good about yourself and this creates positivity.

38. HOW TO BE HAPPY

"Happiness is when what you think, what you say, and what you do are in harmony." (Mahatma Gandhi, Indian Leader)

We need to align all aspects of who we are and what we're about in order to be receptive to happiness. Unless we're tuned in to think, feel and act happy, we probably won't get there. Can we think positively and think ourselves happy? Can we feel happy by relaxing and taking a deep breath? Can we act out happiness by smiling? Some of us can increase our feelings of contentment by carrying out these exercises.

If we never experience the flip-side of happiness, such as sadness, then we wouldn't have the capacity to experience happiness. We need a balance.

ASPIRATIONS. What if we decide that it's more real to aim to be content, joyful, pleased, delighted and cheerful? That sounds like a pretty attractive clutch of feeling states rather than just "being happy" – and it's probably more achievable.

HERE AND NOW. What's the value in brooding over the past, when you can be present in the moment? Use your senses (sight, sound, smell, touch) to value, appreciate and enjoy what's around you.

VALUE WHAT YOU HAVE. If you spend most of your time focused on aspiring to get or achieve something, you fail to enjoy what you have. (See Enjoy What You Have)

FOCUS. Develop an achievable goal and a plan to reach it. Pat yourself on the back when you get there.

PURPOSE. Think about what's important to you or something you strongly believe in, because often we forget what really matters to us. (See Developing Purpose)

JOURNEY. Enjoy the journey rather than being preoccupied with the end result, because the process is often more interesting, involving or inspiring than the final point.

MEANING. Developing meaning in your life can be an important spiritual exercise. A start can be in "being" rather than in "doing".

"HELLO", "THANKS" AND "SORRY". Three underrated words that, in order, allow you to engage with other people, appreciate people and admit when you have made mistakes – all key social communications.

SOCIAL. Humans are social creatures and we all enjoy and benefit from being with other people, whether it's through sports or social activities.

LOVE YOURSELF. Most of us don't allow enough time for self-care, but it's a great feel-good tonic to develop self-confidence, self-worth, self-value and self-appreciation.

POSITIVITY. You can choose to always think of the worst-case scenario or to catastrophize everything ... or you can be realistically hopeful, confident and optimistic. (See Negative Thinking)

LAUGH. Having fun is a great way to generate happiness vibes. We all laugh at different things – what one person finds funny, another might not. But there's a universality in enjoying laughter.

LIFESTYLE. Your body naturally feels good if you get good sleep, exercise and eat a balanced diet. Adopt a healthy lifestyle that your body and mind will appreciate. It might be fun, too.

GIVE AND ASK FOR HELP. It's comforting to know others are there if you need help and similarly it can make you feel good to be able to help others, maybe through homework, shopping or volunteering.

39. ENJOY WHAT YOU HAVE

"Enjoy this moment. For this moment is your life." (Anon)

TV talent shows lure us into a fantasy of achieving fame and fortune overnight. They intoxicate us with the prospect of "making it big" and that's exactly why we watch them and love them! The problem is that part of this fictional dream world stays with us and we begin to feel that "one day very soon" it will be our turn. But that's not life. We end up dreaming our lives away, thinking of a tomorrow that never comes. What we forget about and ignore is ... "today".

If we learn to embrace what we have today, we'll enjoy it more, and probably be much less obsessed with dreams that might never be achieved. When we're on our deathbed, wouldn't it be a waste to be thinking, "I just dreamed and never enjoyed what I had"?

PERSPECTIVE. Put things into perspective so you don't live a life of longing or disappointment.
LIVE IN THE MOMENT. Train your mind and body to use your senses more, to smell the air you breathe, to listen to the world around you, to look beyond what you see, and to feel how your body experiences sensations.
DON'T COMPARE. When you were at school or college, you were probably continually rating yourself against your colleagues, in

sports, exams, etc. This can continue into our later lives. Sure, competition can be positive and motivating. But when you're always comparing yourself to others, you're ignoring yourself.

LIVE FOR YOU. At some point in life you may lose someone close to you who had a huge positive influence on your life and choose to honor them by "living for them". You do a greater honor by "living for yourself" while remembering them.

PARENTAL PRESSURE. We often make choices and decisions in life because we think this is what our parents want of us. In most cases, our parents just want us to be happy and confident.

NOTHING TO PROVE. "Proving" yourself to others may be associated with not having received the praise or attention you sought when you were younger. You don't need to prove anything to anyone ... except yourself.

SHOULD. If you say to yourself, "I *should* do this," then often the word "should" refers to someone else, or a voice, telling you what to do. If you catch yourself saying, "I *should* do this or that," have a think about who's saying "should" here. Is it your parent, school teacher, priest, relative, child or boss?

40. FRUSTRATION

> *"Laughter and tears are both responses to frustration.
> I prefer to laugh, as there is less cleaning up to do afterwards."*
> (Kurt Vonnegut, Author)

We all experience frustration, whether it's concerning something that doesn't work out the way we want it to or not getting something we want. It's frustrating, isn't it?

Frustration is linked to resentment or anger, yet it is often harder to identify because of the varying variables associated with it. For instance, when we're pressured and need to get from A to B quickly, we might get frustrated by traffic or roadworks inhibiting our journey. Yet on another day, with less need to reach B by a certain time, it is less frustrating. And that's because there's always an underlying reason why we feel frustrated.

NEEDS. Frustration occurs in relation to whether your needs are being met. However, evaluate the extent to which your needs *have* to be met, from 1-10 (with "must" at 10) and you'll rarely hit 10.
CONTROL. Frustration can also be impacted by how much control you have in situations. Sometimes you can't control external events, but you can control how you feel, think or react to it.

IMPORTANCE. The more important your task, the greater the frustration if something inhibits it. But is this correctly taken in context? Is it really that important?

REFOCUS. Often a frustration state feels like being trapped. Get out of this trapped state by thinking of something different, or even moving out of your current stressed location, if you can.

BREATHING. When you're frustrated, you're tense. Regulate your breathing: inhale through your nose for a few seconds, hold, then exhale through your mouth slowly.

MUSIC. Listen to music that's calming or takes you back to a familiar, relaxed or altered state.

AVOIDANCE. If you spot a pattern in how your frustration emerges, then find a way to prevent repeating that habit by acting differently next time.

EXPECTATIONS. Is your frustration associated with an unrealistic expectation of yourself or others? Ensure expectations are accurate, reasonable and achievable. Seek clarification or provide confirmation as appropriate.

TIME-KEEPING. If your trigger is linked to being late, how can you reschedule your itinerary to ensure you limit this happening again?

HINDSIGHT. Reflecting on the reasons why certain things frustrate you can help you build a reality check that limits future frustration. If you knew the traffic delay was caused by a horrific accident ahead, would that temper how you felt or reacted?

SETBACKS. These are a necessary part of life that, if you have the appropriate mindset, help you learn and develop.

PERMISSION. Maybe you have a right to be frustrated and it's an appropriate response. But don't beat yourself up by it or be defined by it. It'll pass.

41. PUBLIC SPEAKING ANXIETY

"There are always three speeches for every one you actually gave. The one you practiced, the one you gave, and the one you wish you gave."
(Dale Carnegie, Author and Educator)

A wavering voice, blotchy red face, sweaty palms – these pictures of ourselves increase our fears of public speaking. How we think we will look or come across matters. Sure, we want to speak with conviction and authority, yet this form of "performance anxiety" or negative self-critical thinking often threatens to paralyse us.

Our preoccupation with what others think often ignores the fact that the audience is there because they are interested in us and want to hear us. Our fears are usually overexaggerated – a misdirected or misunderstood perception of the reality.

PRACTISE. You'll feel more confident if you practise your delivery. Know your key messages and your points of emphasis.
BREATHING. Before you begin, take a few deep breaths. Breathe in through your nose and out through your mouth.
STAGE NERVES. These are potentially good! Even the greatest theatre performers can become very nervous before going on stage, but they are able to channel this energy in a positive direction.
INTERACT. Connect with your audience with leading questions or

hypothetical statements. If you are nervous, you could always plant a question with a trusted colleague in the audience.

ANECDOTES. Introduce some stories to illustrate your points. It's often easier to reflect on an anecdote that's slightly off your script, as it brings in a human dimension.

PERFECTIONISM. Avoid trying to be perfect. No one's perfect. Focus on how you can improve from feedback and experience.

SANDWICH. Explain what you're going to talk about, say it, then conclude with a summary of what you've just said.

PRESENTATION AIDS. Avoid reading long chunks of material; keep written material to a minimum and use it as a cue to "explain" rather than "lecture". Writing headings or cues on index cards can help.

COMMUNICATE. If you shift your perception from "talking to" to "communicating with", then it becomes a shared, communal and consensual relationship with the audience.

THREE POINTS. The audience is only going to remember three main points. Nail them.

WHAT IF. Public speaking anxiety is often associated with negative thinking. Try to develop a positive visual image of yourself delivering a great presentation. (See Negative Thinking)

STAND FIRM. Avoid dancing from foot to foot. Keep yourself steady. By all means move about, but when this accentuates what you're saying rather than distracting from it.

PAUSE. Add in moments of quiet. People hear silences. A pause can create a dramatic effect.

SCAN. Your audience will feel connected when you look at them.

PANIC ATTACKS. Nine times out of 10 it won't happen, but it's the fear or threat that triggers the uncertainty. (See Panic Attacks)

SMILE. Feel the positive vibes, embrace this opportunity, go out and give it your best shot, enjoy the experience and smile. It might be your best-ever speech!

42. EMPATHY

"Empathy is about finding echoes of another person in yourself."
(Mohsin Hamid, Author)

One of the most underrated *soft* skills is the ability to empathize with another human being. Characterized by "walking in the shoes of another person", empathy is concerned with developing an understanding, appreciation and awareness of another person's needs and emotions, issues and concerns, motivations and drives. On many levels it's an intuition or a felt-sense, but it can also be learned.

Think about an engaging fiction novel you've read or a captivating movie you've watched. Often you will find that you build up an affinity with the characters, that you developed an empathy for them – you've felt their pain or shared their triumphs. In the real world, empathy follows a similar path, in that you're seeking to experience the world of others, not through your perspective, but through theirs.

UNDERSTAND OTHERS. You get to know people by listening to them, not just by what they say, but through the non-verbal cues of subtle physical responses and body language.

POTENTIAL. Applicable to home and work lives, you develop empathy by helping to fulfil the needs and wants of others, through personal and, in the case of work, professional development.

SUSPEND SELF. Rather than focusing on what you want, stop and consider what others want. This helps you appreciate why people may have different needs or views.

PERSPECTIVE. If you only look through the spectrum of your world, you'll lose out on important information such as the wider landscape around you. You live in relation to others, at home and work. Their perspective counts too.

DIVERSITY. Organizations are waking up to the importance of differences within a team, which help to service different customer needs better. From a personal perspective, learn to appreciate, value and engage with others who are different than you.

RESPECT. As we have our own views and opinions, know that others have their own too. Respect differences so that others respect yours.

INTUITION. People don't always say what they mean and can mask how they show this. Learn to trust and value your instincts about others, but also ask questions to build an understanding of them.

COMPASSION. How can you best communicate your own feelings of compassion, connection, warmth or sympathy to someone who is in pain or has emotional hurt in a way that you'd appreciate if in a similar situation?

CURIOSITY. By learning to be curious about others, you'll learn more about them ... and this will build up your insights about yourself.

NON-JUDGMENTAL. Suspend your own opinion. Whose purpose does judgment or opinion serve?

MODELLING. Think of someone who inspires you. What is it about them that provides this inspiration – is it what they say or what they do?

EMOTIONAL INTELLIGENCE. Empathy is at the heart of emotional intelligence. But you have to know yourself before you can know others. Similarly, you need to be able to love yourself (and all your failings) before you can love others (and all their failings!). (See Emotional Intelligence)

COMMONALITIES. There's more in common between us than what makes us different. There's more that connects us than divides us.

PART FOUR

LIFE EVENTS

43. LIFE CYCLE LOSSES

"Life is like riding a bicycle. To keep your balance, you must keep moving." (Albert Einstein, Theoretical Physicist)

Change is the one constant in life. And change is happening all around us. We start school, form friendships, go to high school, maybe go to college, have relationships, get a job, maybe get married, change jobs, possibly have children, maybe change relationships, move home, deal with bereavements along the way and face the prospect of our own end of life.

While there is a lot of positivity in many of these life stages, there's also an underacknowledged stream of losses. Positive or happy times can mask losses – birthdays represent a loss of youth, a promotion may trigger a loss of a previous work identity, marriage may introduce a loss of being independent, having children may present a loss of freedom, moving home may feel like a loss of your previous social community and so on.

Life becomes about coping better with each loss as it emerges, so that each subsequent loss is managed on its own merit rather than being tinged by the trauma of previous losses.

DENIAL. This is a self-protective mechanism to limit the pain from loss and can be associated with both a desire to "move on quickly" or ignore what's happened.

IMMERSION. Stay in the moment and absorb the impact of the loss. This is when you'll feel the greatest hurt or pain, but it's a way to take stock before you can regroup and muster the strength and power to move on methodically.

ACKNOWLEDGE. Name the loss, how it occurred and the consequences. It's normal to *feel* the loss.

PERSPECTIVE. To understand a loss, put some perspective on its meaning for, and impact on, you.

ACCEPT. As you move through the process, accept what's happened and recognize the changes.

MOURN. Don't force it if it isn't there, but if it is, it's OK to be sad and mourn what's been lost.

MEANING. As you achieve some space from the most painful aspects of the loss, reflect on the positive meanings that could emerge from the loss. This could be about the "silver lining" or the new opportunities that open up.

TRANSFORMATIONAL GROWTH. Embrace the shift that a loss can reformulate into a positive gain. It can sound almost "disrespectful" to seek out a gain from a loss, but it's more disrespectful *not* to acknowledge the learning or opportunities that can emerge. It opens a door that might have felt closed or clears the fog that enveloped us.

In this way, birthdays acknowledge the loss of youth and celebrate the virtue of wisdom and experience. A promotion appreciates the loss of former work identities and revels in the new roles and tasks that provide new friendships and opportunities. Marriage marks the passing of singledom and welcomes a shared life with a partner. And having children erodes previous freedom to introduce a new family of involvement and activity. Every cloud has a silver lining.

44. REDUNDANCY

> "I have been made redundant before and it is a terrible blow; redundant is a rotten word because it makes you think you are useless."
> (Billy Connolly, Comedian, Actor and Musician)

Most of us will be in a job that is made redundant at some time in our lives. This can happen because our employer can't afford to maintain the same number of employees or there's some kind of restructuring. But it can also occur when an organization is taken over or, sadly, if it goes bust. It can have a huge impact on us. So if we're faced with redundancy, we lose the structure and purpose, as well as our work identity. It can also have a massive effect on our finances.

When our employer says they don't have a job for us anymore, it can hurt. We may feel bitter, even devastated. And we'll want to blame someone. We'll think, "After all I gave them, this is the thanks I get." Because we get hit with many reactions to redundancy, we can feel quite vulnerable, as if our stability has gone. We're not feeling grounded anymore, we're floundering about, perhaps all over the place, lacking concentration, purpose and any enthusiasm. We feel totally flat.

THE JOB'S GONE, NOT US. The greatest knock you get is the sense of feeling "redundant" as a person. Well, you're not. It's the job that has been made redundant, not you. You're still here. You still have a lot to offer.

SHARE THE LOAD. It's your job that's gone, so it feels very personal and isolating. It's good to find someone to talk to about how you feel, the frustrations and sense of injustice. Don't bottle it up. (See Therapy)

KNOW THE SCORE. It's important to get as much information about what's actually happened. This helps you process and aids understanding. It might also highlight some options for you – maybe some extra training, a new role elsewhere, outplacement support or a redundancy package?

CUT EXPENSES. You might get a slight financial cushion (redundancy settlement) from your employer or you may not. Either way, it's prudent to draw up a list of the bills you need to pay and how you can cut down on expenses. If you're going to be under financial pressure, contact your creditors, like mortgage or credit card providers. They can usually help you spread or pause payments. (See Debt)

A NEW WAY. Sometimes, being forced into a situation can open up new opportunities you never thought were around. Look beyond your normal field of vision. Is there an opportunity to retrain and do something different, perhaps something you've always hankered for?

BACK TO THE FUTURE. Imagine you're five years in the future from now; what advice might you give yourself?

LEARN FROM OTHERS. If other friends or family have gone through redundancy, it can help to get their perspective. How did they cope? What did they feel? What did they learn from it? What would they advise you?

45. NEW JOB

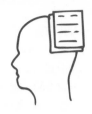

"The future depends on what you do today."
(Mahatma Gandhi, Indian Leader)

Congratulations, you've got a new job! Now the hard bit begins. You'll be excited, itching to get going, but also potentially overwhelmed. You can't do everything at once. There may be a probationary period, which gives you time to settle in, but you'll know people are watching you. By appointing you, people have gone out on a limb to trust that you're the best one for the job. You'll sense this expectation but it needn't paralyse you. Everyone's had to start their job some time.

STATUS QUO. Invest time and assess how the land lies. Stand back and watch and listen, ask questions and invite conversations. Don't rush to act or commit; this is your exploratory phase.

MEET. Get to know key stakeholders, team members, partners and perhaps the people who interviewed you. Understand their roles.

TRUST. There will always be key people who will be "knowers" and "doers", folk you can trust and who will act as a rock of information for connections, internal systems and procedures. Find and nurture them.

DREAM TEAM. Relationships will help or hinder you in a new job. Identify the major influencers who can contribute to you doing your job best, but don't forget to build relationships with peers and people at all levels; everyone needs to be treated with respect.

PROCEDURES. Understand how the organization works by learning the formal protocols so you know the framework within which you can operate.

CULTURE. An organizational culture may be formalized (their mission and vision), but there will be informal aspects as well. Dig beneath the surface to identify the implicit norms, rules and values.

NOT KNOWING. At the start it's normal to feel out of your depth. Resist burning yourself out trying to learn or know everything right away. (See Not Knowing)

DELEGATE. Share the load, but don't abdicate your workload on others. Your team will also want to prove themselves to you. You may need to take a risk initially until trust is earned and evidence of your skills has been demonstrated. (See Delegation)

EXPECTATIONS. Be realistic of what is expected of you, as people may be keen to "test" you or offload their work on you. Underpromise and overdeliver. (See Assertiveness)

CHANGES. Avoid bulldozing in with suggestions of changes unless there's a crisis to solve. Prove first that you're a team player.

BABY STEPS. Resist jumping in with both feet. Manage your workload sensibly.

BOSS. Get to know your boss(es); what are their concerns, issues, priorities and agendas? Try to agree on some initial objectives to focus on. (See Politically Astute)

SOCIAL. Make the most of any social activities to meet your team informally, but don't overdo it. Stay professional yet personable.

IMPRESSION. Make a good first impression. Dress appropriately, show up on time and model a healthy work-life balance.

MENTOR. You may be offered work orientation in the job; don't skip this. There may be a person who is in a more senior position who can be an important role model for you; ask them to be your mentor.

HELP. Know how, when, where and whom you can ask for help. You'll start with a knowledge deficiency and the only way of building on this is to ask questions.

46. RETIREMENT

"The trouble with retirement is that you never get a day off."
(Abe Lemons, Basketball Player and Coach)

After a lifetime of structured employment, it can feel daunting to face the prospect of a time without this routine and a defined work identity. But like many life events, it's a major stage in life we'll all face and one that can present huge opportunities for personal enlightenment, intellectual cultivation ... and fun!

FINANCIAL PLANNING. The most important issue to prepare for is financial stability. If you haven't already, seek independent financial advice on how you can invest or prepare financially. Work out your likely costs and expenditures and assess how best to meet these needs.

TIMING. Based on your financial assets, savings and investments, work out when it might be feasible and practical to retire, factoring in your lifestyle demands and aspirations. Working, say, two years longer might make a big difference in your pension income.

PART-TIME. Many people decide to keep some employment going with part-time work or self-employment. You'll have built up a lifetime of experience; how can you utilize this?

TRANSITION. Preparing for any transition helps, but ultimately it's like moving from one job to another (something you've probably done before), heralding a mix of excitement and anxiety.

PARTNER. Can a partner or loved one help you prepare for or enjoy retirement? It will certainly impact them and they may need to adapt as well!

PURPOSE AND FULFILMENT. What can you do that brings meaning and value to your life now? As you age, you may find you have more interest in spiritual aspirations. Talking about these and exploring your beliefs can help you develop a greater purpose.

HEALTH. Are there any health needs you need to prepare for, including what health care facilities are located nearby?

FAMILY. Do you have an opportunity to help or support your extended family (or maybe you want a break from them!)?

ACTIVITIES. Lots of clubs, societies and special interest groups exist for retired people precisely because there's demand for them. They're great for enhancing your social life, can promote well-being and often provide exercise and health benefits.

VOLUNTEER. There are many ways to give something back and offer your services. It's a great way to make new friends and have fun, too. Helping others will give you a feel-good factor.

ACTIVE MIND. Maintain some intellectual stimulation. Could you enrol in a short course at college, learn a language or skill, teach others, learn a musical instrument or how to sing, or offer some coaching?

EXERCISE. You may have more aches and pains than before, but it shouldn't stop you from exercising. Check with your medical doctor about what would be appropriate for you.

CONTENTMENT. Guard against feelings of isolation, loneliness and depression. Actively manage how you feel by staying positive through how you think or act.

COMMUNICATE. Talk to people – you'll be surprised how interested people are in your rich life experiences and the things you have done in life.

ENJOY. You're embarking on a life stage where you may have choices to do things that you never had before. Lucky you! Have a party!

47. CHILDREN LEAVING HOME

"Home is a place you grow up wanting to leave, and grow old wanting to get back to." (John Ed Pearce, Writer and Columnist)

Parents want to nurture their children to be self-reliant, confident and responsible so they can "fly the nest" and blossom as independent adults. Yet this can also be a great loss to parents.

As young adults prepare to leave home, there will be a mix of excitement and anxiety. Some might breeze through this process, quickly settling into a life with new friends and new experiences. But tied to this will be anxiety about the unknown.

FOR YOUNG ADULTS LEAVING HOME
REASON. Consider your move: is it the right one at the right time for the right reasons? Make a sensible assessment of your motivations. Don't rush into it just because it's an option.

BUDGET. Draw up a budget plan, work out money coming in and budget your costs. Don't forget insurance! It's the one we most often ignore.

TALK. It's important to be open and to talk, not just to your parents whom you're leaving, but also to flatmates or people you're moving in with. It's a two-way street. This helps avoid misunderstandings.

CONNECTION. Moving away from home doesn't mean totally cutting the ties. Maybe it'll be nice if you can keep some regular contact, such as coming around for a specific evening or for Sunday lunch.

FRIENDS. Parents may be quite opinionated about your friends, particularly flatmates, but it's usually with your best intentions in mind. They want you to live with someone "perfect" and no one's perfect! But if your parents criticize them, consider why. They may have a good reason.

HELP. If you find you're struggling, it's OK to ask for help from parents or friends. You're not going to have all the answers. It takes time to learn how it all works. Don't be too proud and stubborn; everyone's been in the same position before.

FOR PARENTS OF YOUNG ADULTS LEAVING HOME

ACCEPTANCE. Accept that this was going to happen someday. Far from being a "bad parent", maybe this is actually what you've been working toward since day one. (See Empty Nest Syndrome)

LISTEN. Listen to any concerns your son or daughter has and give an open, considered response, not one loaded with accusation, opinion and judgment. It'll sound like nagging and they'll ignore you!

CHECKLIST. Help to draft a checklist that can be used to organize the practical and financial concerns that your child may be experiencing.

SUPPORT. Offer to help them move and contribute what you can for the early stages.

INDEPENDENCE. If you invite them to return to "do their clothes washing", you may reinforce dependence and reduce their capacity to take full responsibility of their new lifestyle.

VISITS. Encourage visits home to keep tabs on how things are progressing and learn about using social media.

48. AGEING

"At age 20, we worry about what others think of us.
At age 40, we don't care what they think of us.
At age 60, we discover they haven't been thinking of us at all."
(Ann Landers, Columnist)

We start ageing the moment we are born. It only ends when we die. Lifestyle choices, eating habits, exercise regimes and learning to deal with the stresses and strains of life will all impact positively and will strengthen the body's resilience as we get older.

START EARLY. In your youth, you rarely considered what you'll be like when we are older, yet how you live your life when you're young can impact on how you'll age. If you do not exercise and eat an unhealthy diet when you're young, you may be prone to obesity-related health issues later.

ATTITUDE. The greatest issue is how you look after your body, physically, and how you react to changes psychologically. You can slow the speed of the impact on your mind and body with healthy living, but much is about your personal attitude, accepting what's happening, living with it, embracing it and enjoying it.

CHOICES. You've only got one body and you've only got one life. Sure, you can do whatever you want – it's your choice. You can party 'til dawn every night and it might be fun. But it will catch up with you. It's not to say you can't party. This can be an important part of socialization or relaxation. But all in moderation.

WISDOM. With age comes wisdom and life experience. And you'll find that you can share these resources with family or those younger than you.

PHYSICAL HEALTH. Be sensible and practical, too. You're going to be more prone to sickness and ill health so it's important you have regular checkups with your medical doctor. Your body still values a healthy and nutritious diet and the phrase "we are what we eat" still applies. Likewise, exercise helps to maintain muscles, bones and tissues and fights illness.

BRAIN HEALTH. Your brain can slow down, too, so keeping your mind active can reduce the speed of the slow down, maybe through puzzles, games, sports, reading, crosswords, work (paid or otherwise), quiz shows ... anything that keeps you thinking.

MENTAL HEALTH. Be alert to signs of poor mental health and ask for help early. Isolation can lead to loneliness, which can trigger depression. (See Depression)

POSITIVITY. Having a positive mental attitude helps too, and you really do have a choice in how you see the world around you. It can make a huge difference to see the glass as half full, rather than half empty. (See How to Be Happy)

FINANCES. Where you may struggle in ageing is when you start to lose your health, or start to run out of money, particularly for elder-care services you may require. This is about planning early.

PURSUITS. Activities, hobbies and interests combine to offer some form of exercise, a way you might maintain social contact with people, keep your mind trained and maintain inspiration, motivation and enthusiasm. Maybe this is bowling, badminton, walking, gardening, going on cruises, meeting up with a book club, church or religious groups, or going back to studying or volunteering. Lots of people take up new activities when they retire. You might meet them!

49. RELATIONSHIP BREAK-UP

"I miss your smile ... but I miss mine more."
(Laurel House, Dating Coach)

Despite the best intentions, a relationship can end. It might have been brilliant, the best, but for whatever reason it just didn't work out. It can be devastating. It can shake us to our very core, feeling like we've lost a part of ourselves. It's heart-breaking. One side often feels more hurt than the other, more wronged and more broken.

It can feel like bereavement, and how we process and work through the pain of a relationship break-up often follows the stages of grief. (See Bereavement)

There's no denying that the pain we feel is very personal and unique to us. There's always a reason why relationships end, but sometimes there doesn't seem to be a rational reason and this makes it difficult to make sense of.

RIGHT ONE. It can take time to find "the one", the person you want to spend the rest of your life with. And this can take time, including going through, and ending, several relationships to know what you want or need.

IS IT OVER? There will be lots of distressing emotions experienced. But have you really exhausted the opportunities you have in your relationship? Strong relationships often bond because the people in them have experienced tough times together, through good and bad, and worked through them.

FORGIVENESS. Perhaps there's a time and place, but you will "move on" more easily if and when you can forgive your partner (or yourself) for the end of the relationship. Sure, you won't forget, but you can learn to forgive. The act of forgiveness serves as an important healing process.

OPPORTUNITY. With an ending comes the opportunity of a new beginning. Who's to say that there isn't someone better about to come into your life?

CONNECTION. You may want to hole up, lock the doors and hide away. But this can disconnect you with the world that can become your lifeline. It can also lead to depression. (See Depression) Build your support network with the right people for you.

HEALTH AND FITNESS. When you feel down and lethargic, exercise helps. It can pump nature's own "feel-good" endorphin hormones into you and might enable you to connect with the outside world. Check with your medical doctor before you start exercising.

SHIELD. If you feel bad about yourself, guard against stumbling into negative or destructive behaviors. (See Negative Thinking)

RELATIONSHIP YOYO. If you find yourself continually jumping from one relationship to the next, leaving a trail of "ex's", stop for a moment and consider what's going on. Is this what you really want? What are you gaining and at who's expense? What are you searching for?

POSITIVE MANTRA. Repeat to yourself all the reasons why you know you're a good person. It's about looking after yourself and being kind to yourself. As a human being, you expect to be treated with respect and dignity, not because of what you have done but for who you are.

50. PREGNANCY AND BIRTH

"There is such a special sweetness in being able to participate in creation."
(Pamela S. Nadav, Author and Educator)

The experience of being pregnant can vary from a really positive experience to a painful trauma. If this is your first pregnancy, it can be especially daunting. It can sometimes feel like you are the first person to go through the experience.

While you may appreciate and welcome advice from parents, family and friends, sometimes this can be regarded as imposed instructions, being told what to do or how to feel. Ultimately, this is your pregnancy.

HELPLESSNESS. Partners and close family can feel helpless if their loved one is in pain or things don't quite work out, or they suffer a complication or trauma such as a miscarriage. (See Miscarriage)

ANXIETIES. During the term, you'll experience lots of mixed anxieties: is the baby still breathing, should I be able to feel the baby moving, what should I eat or drink, what effect does stress have on the baby and how should I avoid it, will I be able to cope during the birth and when they emerge out into the world? These fears are normal.

EXTERNALS. These anxieties can be compounded by additional external influences, such as questions about parenting, family or relationship problems, and violence or abuse.

SHARING. Pregnancy and starting a family can be a real test of a relationship. Do you share the same anticipations, hopes, needs, wants and expectations? How are your evolving parenting roles shaping up and do you agree on your plan if you have one?

HORMONES. You may experience postnatal depression, attachment problems or bonding issues. Communicate how you feel or concerns you have to your medical doctor or to the maternity unit of the hospital. They may offer sources of immediate assistance.

PAST. Going through a pregnancy may bring up negative issues from your own childhood. This does not mean you can't be a good parent, but it may mean some therapy would help. (See Therapy)

FINANCES. Anxiety can come from worries about debt and finances, especially with another mouth to feed. It is better to face this head on and to look at what help is at hand or what you need.

PARTNER. Your partner may feel a little pushed aside, so share your thoughts and feelings with them. This can give added reassurance and a sense that you are not on your own.

ISOLATION. If you feel isolated without a partner, are there any family or friends you can speak with or who can offer you their company? A midwife or other hospital staff can be a valuable resource.

BIRTH PLAN. Write down, in advance, a birth plan regarding your choices for the method and location of the birth, different medical interventions anticipated and the support you want. If you have a partner and want them involved, include them in this plan and discuss how they can help implement it.

WORK ISSUES. If you are pregnant and working, get information on what rights you have so that your health can be protected and you are able to work safely without becoming exhausted. Your boss, Human Resources or Occupational Health departments should be able to advise accordingly.

51. EMPTY NEST SYNDROME

> *"However painful the process of leaving home, for parents and for children, the really frightening thing for both would be the prospect of the child never leaving home."*
> (Robert Neelly Bellah, Sociologist)

Empty Nest Syndrome is a phrase used where a parent may experience feelings of loss and sadness when their child leaves home, characterized by a young bird flying away from the nest.

Parents raise children from a point of total dependence to one of independence, yet when that day comes, when the child is grasping that independence and leaves home, it can generate very strong feelings of loss. They've been central to your home life. It's just not the same without them. It might feel a bit like bereavement and it can take time to adjust and accept.

ACCEPT. Of course you may miss your child and worry about them. That's perfectly natural. But you need to accept this is happening. Self-care. Look after yourself. Appreciate you're going through this life event and understand you still need to care for yourself, even if you're not caring for your child in quite the way you did.

NO CHANGE. What doesn't ever change is that you will *always* be the parent!

COMPARISONS. Don't compare what it was like for you when you left home. What's happening here is unique and so you need to appreciate this from your child's point of view.

OTHER EVENTS. The time when your child leaves home may coincide with the need to support, look after or care for elderly relatives or parents. You might also find you're experiencing menopause. These are big life changes and you need to give some space to them.

GUIDANCE. Sometimes it can help to see yourself as less of the "parent who makes rules" to someone who can provide guidance and coaching. It's an opportunity to develop a new relationship with your child.

RESPECT AS ADULTS. It can be tempting to stay in the parent/child mode and continue to regard your child as your baby, but they're adults now. Show respect and treat them as independent adults.

KEEP IN TOUCH. Stay connected via social media, texts and emails, as well as the good, old-fashioned face-to-face catch up, maybe tempting them back with a hearty Sunday lunch or weekend activity.

BEGINNINGS. Now is a time to give time back to you. Is there a hobby, interest or pastime you've always dreamed of?

PARTNERS. When children have left home, and for people with a partner, you might find the relationship changes, sometimes for the better, and sometimes exposing problems.

DELAY CHANGES. It takes time to adapt to the changes and understand how they affect you. It might be prudent to delay making any big changes until you've become used to the new scenario.

SUPPORT. Many people experience this empty nest syndrome. It might help to speak with a therapist to give yourself time and space to explore what the changes mean. (See Therapy)

STAY POSITIVE. The feelings of sadness and loss should be temporary and you can reduce this time by focusing on the positives. (See Negative Thinking)

52. PARENTING CHILDREN AGES 0-11

"Parenting isn't a practice, it's a daily learning experience." (Anon)

Your world will likely be dominated by your child's early development and most of what you go through now is not so much about guiding for the future, but coping with the present.

After nine months of pregnancy spent planning, worrying and not sleeping, you begin to realize that this will continue with more of the same – more planning, more worrying and more issues with sleep. Yet it's never quite like you imagined and with the first born, it's a completely new experience. Your body takes over and you are at the mercy of the medical profession to nurture you, and your baby, through birth and recovery. The birth itself can be a difficult time, both physically and emotionally. New skills are required as your baby develops into a child and approaches the teenage years.

SLEEP. It's very unlikely that you'll get your regular and routine blissful sleep. It's more likely to be grabbing a few hours here and a few hours there.

SUPPORT. With your mind totally preoccupied with the baby, you can often overlook sources of help and support, from medical post-natal support, your medical doctor and family and friends.

PARTNERS. Remember to include your partner, if you have one, or the other parent of the child. If you are no longer together, try to negotiate access for the sake of the child.

SHOW THE LOVE. Babies and children can feel the love you express, so build this through physical nurturing, play time, communicating that you love them and demonstrating this.

EMOTIONAL TANKS. Think of children as having emotional reservoir tanks. These need topping up through the expressions of love you show them.

RIGHT THE WRONGS. Catch your child doing something right rather than criticizing something they've done wrong. They learn more from positive reinforcement than negative reinforcement.

QUALITY TIME. Learn active listening, not just what you hear in terms of words, but the sentiment or expression, intention and meaning behind them. A child who feels listened to is likely to be more open with you and better able to express themselves. (See Empathy)

BOUNDARIES. Without any rules, children quickly learn that anything goes. But manage boundaries and you give children security and safety. After all, what would happen if you didn't give a toddler the boundary rule of staying away from the road or the fireplace or a water hazard?

CONSISTENCY. Boundaries only work with consistency, so *no* today means *no* tomorrow. This is most often broken by one parent setting one rule and the other parent changing it. This gives confusing messages to the child.

PRIORITIZE. You can't win every battle, but you can focus on the really important ones.

LEVEL IT. When you communicate with the child, eye contact helps offer reassurance and focus. Seeing you offers confidence and stability, especially if you physically get down to the level of the child.

53. PARENTING CHILDREN AGES 12-18

"Tell me and I forget, teach me and I remember, involve me and I learn."
(Benjamin Franklin, US Statesman)

The scope of parenting continually shifts. There's no fixed point. It's difficult to get right, too.

Sometimes we think that our children are not able to understand reasoning and problem-solving and certainly can't understand adult emotions, but this is often not true. Our children usually know when something is wrong, or if they have upset us or behaved badly, even if they can't verbally express to us what the problem is.

When we consider parenting, we fixate on "how to do things better", but much credit should be given to all parents who juggle and muddle through the experience and learn what needs to be done.

CLEAR, CONSISTENT AND FIRM. This is especially important when there are two parents involved. If you don't agree on and share the rules of parenting, then young people can be confused and may play you off against each other, even if they don't realize they're doing it.

PARTNERS. If you're in a relationship with someone, nurture and develop this, too. Some couples come with different expectations of being a parent, so it's crucial that you communicate and understand how to maintain a united front for parenting.

HEAR. Listening to young people is an underrated skill. It's about how you hear them and show you are attentive to them.

COMMUNICATION. This is how you express your emotions to them, share your thoughts, teach them about reasoning and logic, develop a thirst for learning and knowledge, guide them through behaviors that are acceptable (and what's not) and ultimately how they communicate with other human beings.

BOUNDARIES. Young people push against boundaries, not because they want to provoke you (though sometimes it might seem like this), but because it's their way of striving for independence and also to test whether you care.

REASONING. If you need to challenge or criticize, make sure the child is clear that although you may be unhappy with their behavior, you still love and care for them. Invite them to talk openly about their behavior and the reasons behind any sanctions.

FLEXIBILITY AND ADAPTABILITY. Prioritize which are the non-negotiable boundaries or rules. Be flexible and patient, but firm and consistent as well. Some things may be negotiable, but it's up to you to determine what's negotiable, when and why. For instance, they can play on the computer after cleaning their room. This generates a reward for responsible behavior and helps them understand what rules are and why.

PARENT FIRST, FRIEND SECOND. Young people need boundaries, guidance and encouragement when exhibiting positive behavior or actions and reprimanded when they've done something wrong. In time, you might find you're changing from being the "person in charge" to being a sort of life coach or consultant!

MODELLING. All the qualities you want your child to possess will most likely emerge from your ability to model them. Practice what you preach.

TEENAGE BEHAVIOR. As young people grow, their bodies are swamped with hormones, which often explains confrontational behavior. It's not personal – it's hormones.

RESPECT. Treat them as mini-adults. Do this by respecting them as individuals with their own views and opinions, even if you don't agree with them. If you offer them responsibility, they'll feel worthy of taking responsibility. If you treat them as significant, they'll act as significant people.

SELF-CARE. You can often get so caught up in the roles and responsibilities of being a parent that you lose sight of your own needs, wants and self-care.

54. BEREAVEMENT

"Death is the last intimate thing we ever do."
(Laurell K Hamilton, Author)

Any form of loss can be painful, which includes anything from ending a relationship or losing a job to the death of someone close to us. The process of grieving can take time, from a year to a lifetime, but everyone's different and so are the circumstances. What is universal is that the pain hurts.

Grieving is not just about one feeling, but a whole succession of feelings, and the sequence in which we experience them is often unique. Some of us go through each stage sequentially, while others dot around or can get stuck in a certain stage.

THE STAGES OF BEREAVEMENT
SHOCK – Numbness and Denial
Immediately after the death or loss, you'll experience a sense of shock, not really believing it's happened to you. After the initial shock, you probably won't believe it, denying what's happened.
ANGER – Resentment and Aggression
Anger is a normal response to loss. It's part of the grieving process. You might find yourself angry at people around you, your family, medical doctor or hospital ("Why couldn't more have been done?").

You'll want to blame people, maybe yourself or (and this is surprisingly common) feel angry at the person who's died ("How could you do this to me?").

SORROW – Despair and Guilt

This can be a gut-wrenching stage when, after the funeral or memorial service and the well-wishers have disappeared, you realize that "this is it", that you have to adapt to a new life without the person. You may feel some sense of guilt too ("I wish I'd seen them more or been a better person to them").

DEPRESSION – Apathy and Disconnection

After the initial raw feelings of pain have subsided, you may find yourself feeling pretty down, a sort of depression. This is normal. You probably won't feel very sociable or be bothered to do anything. As some time might have passed now, friends might have stopped checking to see if you're OK. You may feel a sense of being on your own with it all. But grieving takes time.

ACCEPTANCE – Revival and Reconnection

You know you've moved on when you start to get out more, get energy or enthusiasm back, and reconnect with people and life in general. You still remember the person, but without the really debilitating feelings you had at the start. This isn't a fixed point and you may still have bad days when triggers bring back situations and memories. But in time, these memories will become less sad and perhaps tinged with a happy reflection of the good times you had with the person.

TRANSFORMATION – Growth and Enlightenment

This is not a stage everyone experiences, so don't expect it. But some people find that after the trauma of loss, they find a change in something about themselves – their values, a different perspective on life, more meaning or a change in their belief system. This can feel like a positive that has emerged from a negative. Life can be strange.

SELFCARE IS VITAL. Be good to yourself. Look after yourself. Eat well, exercise, try to have a decent amount of sleep and tentatively engage with other people. Avoid using alcohol as a mood enhancer. **IT'S GOOD TO TALK.** You may want some space to be on your own, and that's fine. But sometimes you may need to express what you're feeling. The key is finding the "right people to talk to" – a friend or family member, or perhaps someone objective like a therapist. (See Therapy)

Things will get better in time.

55. MIDLIFE CRISIS

> "Midlife is when you reach the top of the ladder
> and find it was against the wrong wall."
> (Joseph Campbell, Mythologist and Writer)

Life, from the cradle to the grave, is a series of stages or cycles. And we grow, develop, learn and experience one after the other. Reaching midlife is one of these stages.

Feelings associated with this stage can be frightening and painful. It can feel like a door is slowly closing. But if a door can close, it can open, too, and we can be presented with the opportunity to make new decisions about our life. A midlife crisis can be a complex mix of issues: fear of growing older, worry about our mortality and dying, anxiety about missed opportunities, angst about unresolved issues from the past, frustration about how things are at the moment, and tension surrounding menopause. These issues reveal powerful emotions – fear, worry, anxiety, angst, frustration and tension. (See Managing Emotions)

At the midlife point in our lives, we might be yearning to do some reinventing of ourselves, to "get back on track" and "live again". Families and jobs might have pushed us on a well-worn path for many years, and suddenly we realize we might not have long left on this earth, so we want to make the most of things. This is actually why a midlife crisis should really be referred to as a "midlife rebirth".

CRISIS, WHAT CRISIS? Understand what the fears and worries are about and scrutinize why you feel them.

ACCEPT. It's impossible to have planned one's life completely. Your life evolves through circumstances and opportunities often beyond your control. Life weaves its own complex tapestry.

RE-ASSESS. It's probably healthy to re-assess how things are going for you. But often you might wait for a stagnant point for such self-examination. Perhaps there are choices you can make *now* to offer you a better life?

PLAN. If you just see a hazy, unclear future, then start making some plans. Do you want to spend more time with your family (or less)? Or what about if you cut your hours and work part-time so you could take up a new hobby? What's your financial position and how does understanding this allow you to make new decisions about what you can do?

EMBRACE. There's a great deal to be thankful for at this stage in life. You will have accumulated huge gains in knowledge, confidence, maturity, experience and skills, maybe even savings – things you didn't have when you were young. How can you utilize these gains?

HEALTH. At the midlife point, your body won't be as flexible and spritely as it once was. It's never too late to adopt a healthy lifestyle and there's loads of evidence that proves the feel-good benefits of a better diet, regular exercise, stopping smoking and moderating alcohol consumption.

ASSERT. If you've put up with circumstances that you were not happy with, perhaps you have a chance to identify what you really want and need and make a conscious decision to put yourself first. What do you need and want in life *now*?

CONSEQUENCES. It's your life, and you have choices. But with choices come consequences. Think before you act, especially before you quit your job or end a relationship. This might be the right thing to do, but don't act without considering all the consequences. (See Therapy)

56. BEREAVEMENT THROUGH SUICIDE

"When people kill themselves, they think they're ending the pain, but all they're doing is passing it on to those they leave behind."
(Jeannette Walls, Writer)

Suicide is still a taboo subject, yet it's surprisingly common. For those of us left behind after a suicide, often we do not want, or feel able, to talk about it because it can create feelings of guilt and prompt questions over whether something could have been done to prevent it. Why did they do it? It's important to know and accept that sometimes in such a situation, there was absolutely nothing we could have done.

UNIQUENESS. Sometimes the action of suicide can originate from a feeling of being utterly trapped with no way out, an excruciating sense of hopelessness and helplessness, or a desire to escape intense psychological or emotional pain. It can also be linked to illness and disability, addictions, depression and self-harming behaviors. It might be intentional, but it could be accidental.

PERMANENCE. It's a very permanent solution to what might be a temporary problem. It's just that some people don't see their predicament as temporary.

CHOICE. Some people consider suicide to be a person's choice or right. But this can be really difficult to hear, as a suicide can cause a feeling of terrible rejection; a rejection of you and a rejection of life. You're left behind to cope with the feelings of loss and your own pain, guilt and heartache. Like any bereavement, it can take a long time to make sense of what's happened and to cope with the after-effects. (See Bereavement)

COMMUNICATIONS. As well as trying to make sense of a suicide ourselves, in a family context you may also have to find the words to explain what's happened to a range of other people, including extended family, work colleagues, friends and children. Each set of people will feel a different connection to the deceased, but will share a similar sense of confusion and loss.

PROTOCOLS. A suicide may prompt involvement by the police and a funeral may be delayed by an inquest. This can add to the tension surrounding the loss. Keep in touch with the authorities so they can clarify procedures and protocols.

DISCUSSION. Talking about a death through suicide can be really tough, particularly when explaining it to a child. Be open and honest about what's happened, give some suitable context, encourage an expression of feelings and, in time, cherish the good memories and stories about the person. If a child asks, "Why?", respond by asking, "What do you think?". You can then craft the conversation, and your answer, around their response. Seek out the charities that specialize in support for children bereaved by suicide.

UNKNOWNS. Sometimes, you'll never truly know why someone chose to end their life. It's OK to acknowledge any frustration and angst associated with this. But ultimately, it's about accepting you'll never fully know why.

57. TRAUMATIC EVENTS

"Hardships often prepare ordinary people for an extraordinary destiny."
(C.S. Lewis, Novelist)

We all respond to traumatic events in different ways. Some build up resilience from previous events, but for others, one event can trigger more severe conditions such as post-traumatic stress disorder. Even people who regard themselves as having a "strong personality" don't necessarily fare better than those who don't.

People who experience a traumatic incident sometimes experience a series of psychological and physical symptoms. These are often normal responses to abnormal events and usually subside in time. The psychological symptoms include numbness, anxiety, guilt, anger, shock, low mood, social withdrawal, flashbacks and avoiding reminders associated with the event. Physical symptoms include poor concentration, fatigue, sleep problems and nightmares, feeling "on edge", neck tension, aches and pains.

TIME. It really does take time. But if, after a month, you're still affected by the event, then it might be prudent to visit your medical doctor or refer yourself to a trauma therapist.

RECONNECT. The temptation may be to withdraw from normal activities, but that can make you feel more isolated. Keep up social contact and re-engage with people close to you.

ROUTINE. Although your mind may become fixated on what's happened, keep to a regular routine including sleep, a good diet and exercise, as this gives structure, purpose and self-motivation.

WORK. You might find you will be unable to go to work in the short term and indeed, there can be good reason to have a short break and recharge your batteries. But going back to work gives you a connection with your work colleagues and a routine. If the trauma happened at work, you may need to explore how best to reintegrate back to work. Your boss, Occupational Health or Human Resources departments may be able to help.

POSITIVE ACTIVITIES. If you enjoy non-work activities, such as a sport, hobby or pastime, then re-engaging in them can help.

AVOID SELF-MEDICATING. Drinking alcohol and taking drugs may give a sense of a temporary reprieve, but long term they often worsen the effects of trauma by making you feel depressed, anxious, tired and lonely.

ACKNOWLEDGE. Feelings and emotions often increase in intensity, but this is normal. You may experience sudden emotional outbursts, but acknowledging this as part of the process will help you release and ventilate emotions and prevent them from building up inside you.

DENIAL. The majority of people will experience some trauma symptoms for a short period of time and these will lessen. Some may experience absolutely nothing. This can be normal too, but it's worth monitoring how you react and to be on guard that you're not denying any adverse responses.

SELFCARE. Create some space where you can relax, take some time out and monitor your own needs.

POST-TRAUMATIC GROWTH. Many people who have gone through a horrific experience often find that their perspective in life changes. They value things differently and appreciate life more. This is an unexpected and sometimes positive consequence of a trauma.

58. MISCARRIAGE

"But love is born in life and death cannot end it."
(Mette Ivie Harrison, Author)

A miscarriage can be devastating. Hopes, dreams and aspirations come crashing down with a huge weight of loss, sadness and grief. It doesn't really make any difference if it's the first miscarriage or not, the effect can be traumatic. And it's the sudden enforced end to that connection that hurts, physically and emotionally.

What sets this apart from other forms of bereavement is that we are grieving for someone we have never known, a life that has never lived and our lost life as the parent of that child.

MARK. There are different ways to mark this experience. For some it's just a word in a diary, or you may want to mark this more tangibly or physically, perhaps planting a tree or visiting a special place that has meaning for you, or whatever helps you create a memory place.
TALK. Many people don't want to talk to others about miscarriage. It's just too painful. It means facing the fact that the child that could have been, never will be. Therapy may help to give you the space to ventilate your feelings and emotions. (See Therapy)
PARTNER CONNECTION. Miscarriage can be tough on relationships. Find some way through with your partner. Some people have a "fix it" approach, but this isn't about fixing things. Some may want to get on and move on, but it might not be that easy.

Everyone has a different way of dealing with such events, so it's crucial that you can speak to your partner about what you're feeling and how it's affecting you.

GRIEVE. Allow yourself the choice of whether you want to grieve or not. It might not be something you want to do right now, but it might be important later. (See Bereavement)

WOMEN POWER. It might help to connect with or group together some of your female friends. Not that men won't understand, but you can derive a connection or solidarity from other women that is difficult to explain.

FUTURE LOVEMAKING. Having sex the next time might feel a bit strange. After all, it may have led to the pregnancy that led to the miscarriage (notwithstanding fertility treatment) ... so you may associate sex with painful memories. Reassure your partner you're not rejecting them.

WHAT NEXT? After getting the OK from your medical doctor, you can usually try for another pregnancy as soon as your next menstrual cycle. Your fertility is actually highest within the first six months of a miscarriage. But you may also decide not to proceed with another pregnancy.

TLC. You need to look after yourself, even if you don't feel like it. It'll help you get through it better. Allow yourself to grieve, but also to exercise regularly, eat a healthy diet and rest. You still need to eat, wash, get up in the morning and live your life.

59. PREPARING FOR DYING

"We begin to die as soon as we are born, and the end is linked to the beginning."
(Manilius, Poet)

Facing death allows us to plan to make it as manageable as possible, to minimize suffering and generate an opportunity for closure, peace and an ending. For those left behind, our planning may help them better deal with our death and get through their grief.

Preparing for dying has the benefit of allowing us to feel settled and content that things have been dealt with and we're not leaving any loose endings or unresolved issues.

LEGAL ISSUES. If you don't have a will, then complications can arise with your estate. It's not expensive to make a will and you can make changes as long as you're fit to do so. Do you have a power of attorney or someone appointed to act on your behalf if you become unable to do so yourself?

WISHES. It can help others to be aware of what your plans are for when you die. This gives them a chance to make their own preparations if your decisions impact on them.

FUNERAL PLAN. It might feel a bit strange to plan your own funeral, but if you do so, you'll have a structure in place that suits your personality and the funds you have available. By planning for this and knowing the details in advance, you may feel at peace.

LEGACY. How do you want to be remembered? It can be a grounding experience to write out a summary of your life, the good and the bad, the hopes and the dreams, the funny times and the happy times. Who knows, it could be a bestseller!

EXPECTATIONS. If you have an illness that's going to end your life, it's helpful to understand what the actual process of dying will be. How will the illness escalate, will you have sufficient pain relief, will you be in hospital, and how will your mind and body be affected?

GRIEVE. Grieving is considered a process people go through when others die. But it's also about how you grieve for yourself, for the ending of your life. This is particularly relevant if and when you get a diagnosis for a terminal illness and you're faced with the clock ticking away. (See Bereavement)

SOMEONE ELSE DYING? It can be difficult to know what to say. Be up-front and open. Say you feel squeamish or uncomfortable or tongue-tied if you are. Just being there can bring enormous comfort and support. Ask if they really want you to be popping in at all visiting hours! It should not be about what we want, but about what suits them.

PROGNOSIS. Some want to know the details: what's the illness, how it will affect us and what's the prognosis? But others don't. Some of us just want to enjoy the time we have left without focusing on the details, to laugh with friends, to keep our routines going and to enjoy our families.

MORTALITY. When confronted by your own mortality, it can raise deep questions that may not be easily answered. Seek solace or guidance from a religious leader or therapist.

PART FIVE

PERSONAL LIFE
MANAGEMENT

60. STRESS

"If being stressed burned calories, I'd be a supermodel." (Anon)

We need pressure in our lives to motivate and stimulate us to do things. Most of the time, pressure is good for us. But if the pressure we experience is persistent or beyond our coping levels, then it's likely to shift and cause us "dis-stress". However, we're all different; what's stress to one person is positive pressure to another.

In the UK, the Health and Safety Executive (HSE)* published "stress standards", and while this is geared toward the workplace, it has relevance to our personal lives as well. Six core clusters identify key sources of stress:

DEMANDS. Do you have an excessive workload or too much to deal with? Home, relationship and family demands apply here too. Match what is required of you to what you can cope with, delegate or share the load, change work patterns to suit you and maintain a realistic pace.

CONTROL. Do you have sufficient control or power over what you do? Are others diverting your time? Find ways to assert your rights and needs. (See Assertiveness)
Take ownership and ensure that others are clear about your responsibilities and your need to have control over what you do.

SUPPORT. Is there enough support around you to achieve what's required of you? Identify the resources you need to achieve your task. Seek out the motivation, inspiration and encouragement you need. Be open to asking for (and offering) help, and identify and communicate your needs. (See Asking For Help)

RELATIONSHIPS. Relationships are tough to manage (at home and work) with often-competing needs and wants. Understand others (empathy) and build positive relationships. Create an environment that avoids conflict and assert what constitutes unacceptable behavior. (See Managing Conflict)

ROLE. With often-conflicting demands, be clear about your roles and responsibilities; know what's required of you and where you fit in. This applies as much to being a manager as being a parent.

CHANGE. The only thing that's constant about change is change itself. Learn to "go with the flow", adapt to what goes on around you and build in some flexibility for change. Communicate changes and encourage others (especially at work) to keep you informed of changes.

Beyond the HSE "stress standards", you can also learn how to manage your own stress response:

EMOTIONAL COMPASS. Understanding the emotion that alerts you to feelings of stress often helps to identify the source of stress, which then allows you to take action. (See Emotional Intelligence)

ACT. Many people know they're stressed and the causes of their stress, but choose to do nothing. Doing something is often better than doing nothing.

FEELING. If you can't change the situation, you can change how you feel about the situation.

EXERCISE. If you are able to, you'll feel more robust, mentally strong and resilient if you exercise. (See Exercise)

PEOPLE POWER. A network of friends allows you to make social connections, unwind and de-stress.

EMPOWER. What can you do today to take back control of your life?

It's good to talk. A therapist is independent, impartial and skilled at helping you find solutions to problems. Therapy may help you find ways to better manage stress in the future.

TIME FOR *ME*. So much of life can be about doing stuff for others, especially in a job or with family demands. So it's important that you can build in some regular "me time".

LEARN. Nurture and feed your mind to help you more intelligently deal with stress in the future. If you can expand your horizons, it gives you more choices about how you interpret and respond to stress.

BE POSITIVE. Do you seem to attract stress? Being negative can give you a "doom and gloom" attitude. (See Negative Thinking)

MANAGE EXPECTATIONS. Sometimes there's nothing you can do. If your employer's making jobs redundant, you might have no control over this. Maybe the best solution is just to "hang on in there"... or "get out" and take control. (See Political and Economic Uncertainty)

* http://www.hse.gov.uk/stress/standards/

61. ASKING FOR HELP

"Nothing makes one feel so strong as a call for help."
(Pope Paul VI, Leader of the Catholic Church)

Help is as much to do with asking for it as well as giving it. They're different sides of the same coin. It's difficult to be able to ask for help if we don't make ourselves open to helping others. But sometimes it can be more difficult to ask for help. Perhaps we feel we'll appear weak or lose face; that we need to be strong and "ride out the storm". But if this book seeks to achieve anything, it's to empower you to make choices and decisions about you and your world that enable you to live a better life. And being able to ask for help is a key part of achieving this.

KNOW YOURSELF. You need to be able to know your triggers and drives, what makes you happy or what makes you sad, to know your stresses and strains and how you react to stress and difficult times.
EMOTIONS. Know what emotions mean to you and the reasons behind your emotional reactions. (See Managing Emotions)
CLARIFY. Ask yourself questions about what you need and simplify the key issues for you. This can help you focus on finding the right person to give you the support you need.
CONTROL. People often think they lose control if they ask others for help. But you're doing the opposite; you're taking back control. We all need help some time.

RESILIENCE. Sure, we can "roll with the punches" and endure the tough times, which is all about learning to be resilient. But you also need to know when "enough is enough". Everyone has their limits. (See Resilience)

WHO. Identify a mentor or someone you respect and start with them. Even if they are not knowledgeable about your particular question, often a good listener is all you need.

REJECTION. An inhibitor to asking for help is that we fear rejection by the person we ask, or feel we're being a burden. This feeling is usually unfounded.

STRESS. What's pressure and motivation to one person is excessive stress to another. Understand your stress "hot-spots" and how you can manage them better. (See Stress)

WRITING. If you can't say what's going on for you, try writing it down in your own way. Write it as you see things, or maybe as a poem, or even a fictitious short story – just get it down on paper.

THERAPY. Sometimes it's difficult to find the right words to describe how you feel. Consider seeing a therapist to help you find the solutions to your problems. (See Therapy)

HELP SOMEONE. If you're struggling to ask for help, help someone else. Then you'll see how solutions can be found.

MODEL IT. Make "asking for help" an encouraged and acceptable part of your language at home or culture at work.

62. DEBT

"There is scarcely anything that drags a person down like debt."
(P.T. Barnum, Businessman and Showman)

Debt is the borrowing of money from a person or organization that has to be repaid at a future date, usually with interest added. Our attitude to debt should be determined by our financial circumstances, i.e., what we can afford. But debt can creep up on us. Problems can occur when there's an imbalance between money coming in, what we earn, and what goes out, in terms of bills, debt interest and expenditures.

Debt can be triggered by illness, job loss and also a denial of financial responsibilities. As our debt burden increases, it's not uncommon for people to hide this from others, especially partners and family, perhaps pretending there isn't a problem. But something often snaps and we'll have to admit the financial mess we're in and do something about it. We might have feelings of guilt and shame, worry and anxiety, or we might be embarrassed that we've failed to prevent it from happening. The key is resolving the current crisis and planning for a stable financial future.

Please note: We strongly recommend that you seek independent debt advice. The brevity of this chapter means we can only offer basic guidance, which may not cater to your circumstances, and is provided for information purposes only.

PRIORITIZE DEBT. Deal first with the debt that poses the greatest risk or has the most significant consequences, such as the risk of court action or losing your home.

TALK TO CREDITORS. If you alert creditors early enough, they might be able to allow you to renegotiate more manageable payment terms and stave off any action.

CHECK LIABILITY. Make sure you really do have liability for the debt. Don't assume a demand is correct until you've checked it to be accurate.

MAXIMIZE INCOME. Check that you're getting the income you are due, including benefit entitlements, social security payments, tax credits, overtime and expenses settled.

MINIMIZE EXPENDITURES. Brutally cut down on expenditures. You can do without trips to the cinema or meals out temporarily if it resolves your debt crisis.

ORGANIZE. Methodically keep records and track what you owe against what you can afford so you can achieve a clearer assessment of the situation.

REFINANCE. Is refinancing an option? It can be a way to borrow at lower rates than other forms of credit.

CONSOLIDATE. It may help to pool all debts into one managed debt repayment plan.

HANG IN THERE. It can take time to get back onto a level footing. Several years is not unusual. You should be realistic about how long it might take.

PLAN. As you emerge out of the debt gloom, you'll benefit from a new and more structured approach to personal financial management. The key is learning from the past and protecting yourself for the future.

63. THERAPY

"If you break your knee, you have therapy for your knee, and it's the same with your heart."
(Toni Braxton, Singer-Songwriter)

Counselling or coaching is a support intervention involving a professional who can offer an impartial, independent and confidential perspective on issues you're experiencing. This might be about distressing things that have happened or painful feelings that are affecting you. If this is your first time, you may feel anxious, wondering what to say, how it will affect you and when you'll feel better. And because it might mean talking about painful issues, it won't be easy.

It's not the therapist's job to tell you what your problem is and what you should do about it. They're a facilitator who will ask questions, prompt a bit and explore, but only in a way that enables you to work out what's going on and achieve the progress or resolution you seek. While there are different forms of therapy, research suggests it is the quality of the relationship you have with the therapist that matters most.

DECISION. The first big step is deciding to act and see a therapist. Various professional bodies have directories of registered therapists. Most require their members to be listed on a professional register, so check out the requirements in your country.

CHOOSING. Shortlist a few therapists who sound right and either phone or make an appointment to see them. Some offer a free first introductory session to help you decide if they're right for you. It's all about gelling and feeling comfortable with your therapist, so it's OK to decide not to see one that doesn't feel right.

PREPARATION. Before your appointment, it might help to write down some of the things you want to talk about. It doesn't have to be neat and in order and no one's going to read it – it's more as a guide for you.

COMMITMENT. Therapy usually takes longer than a single session, though sometimes that's all you'll need. Otherwise, you may need to commit to working with your therapist over a number of appointments.

ENGAGEMENT. Once you're happy with your choice of therapist, it's over to you. If you feel they're not asking enough questions, tell them. Similarly, if you feel they're jumping in too much, ask for a bit more space! It's about finding the balance in giving you the freedom to talk about stuff with just the right amount of reflecting, prompting and engagement from the therapist.

DURATION. Most sessions last between 50 minutes and one hour. It's up to you how often you visit your therapist, though they may make suggestions. Most will opt for a weekly session. And you'll probably know when you've made sufficient progress to not need to continue any more. It might be four sessions or 12 or 20 – whatever suits you. Some people worry about becoming dependent on therapy. This is always something worth discussing with the therapist.

Therapy is about finding *your* solutions to *your* issues, empowering you to make decisions, building you up to feel stronger, more resilient and better able to cope with life's issues.

64. SLEEPING

*"Sleep is that golden chain that ties
health and our bodies together."*
(Thomas Dekker, Dramatist)

The sleep we need varies throughout life. Babies and young people need more of it than adults and those in their 60s and 70s may need even less. We all want a good night's sleep and it can be really frustrating when we don't get it. This frustration can feed its own insomnia. It can be a vicious circle.

Insomnia can be caused by changes in routine or lifestyle, stimulants, illness, stress, anxiety and depression. However, there are more severe sleep disorders and when these are linked to psychological or physical issues, it's best to get these checked by your medical doctor. Sleep is a good mental health barometer.

PREPARATION. As you count down the hours before sleep, build in a "wind-down" period where you start to slow down your activity.

EAT EARLY. Having a meal just before bedtime can affect sleep, as the body is actively processing and digesting food. Eat your evening meal several hours before bedtime.

EXERCISE. As long as you are able to do so safely (and your medical doctor agrees), regular exercise is important for physical and mental health. It helps to achieve a natural tiredness at the end of the day. The only exception is not to exercise too close to the time you want to sleep, as your body needs time to calm down and relax. However, having sex can aid sleep. (See Exercise)

READING. For some, reading helps to feel sleepy. But others can get so engrossed that they don't want to stop until they've finished the book!

TV. While it's often regarded as relaxation, watching TV in bed can keep you awake. Limit watching TV to outside your bedroom.

CAFFEINE. There's caffeine in tea, coffee, fizzy drinks, hot chocolate and even some herbal drinks. Caffeine is a stimulant and causes increased alertness. Having caffeine in a drink before bedtime can impair sleep. If you drink too much during the day, it can reduce your sleep quality.

ALCOHOL. This is also a stimulant and while often consumed to aid relaxation, it can interfere with your sleep patterns and make you more likely to wake up during the night.

ROUTINE. Stick to a set pattern of sleep and you'll maintain regular sleep cycles.

MINDFULNESS. Meditation helps to zone out into a place of relaxation. It's a way to focus on your breathing, become grounded and create an inner peace.

BREATHING. Even without meditation, you can learn to regulate your breathing in bed, taking long slow breaths, focusing on how this feels, listening to your breathing and relaxing.

RELAX. Chill out with a bath, have a hot non-caffeinated drink, listen to calming music or all three!

THERAPY. If you have worries or fears that are keeping you awake, it may help to see a therapist. (See Therapy)

65. EXERCISE

"To enjoy the glow of good health, you must exercise."
(Gene Tunney, World Heavyweight Boxing Champion)

It is widely recommended by health practitioners that adults engage in moderate intensity exercise for 20-30 minutes a day at least five days a week (that gives us two days off each week!). Children and young people need to aim for about 60 minutes a day.

Exercise can be fun, engaging, stimulating, help you sleep better, reduce how you respond to stress and generally make you feel better about yourself. It's a no-brainer.

If you spend a proportion of your time exercising now, you'll build up a reserve of fitness, which will reduce the potential for the aches and pains you might otherwise suffer from later in life.

DOCTOR. If you haven't exercised for some time or you have a medical condition, make an appointment with your medical doctor. They will determine what exercises might be safe and appropriate. Suddenly leaping into high-energy exercise could do more harm than good.

WALK THE TALK. Walking is probably the most accessible form of exercise around and cheap! Walk at a brisk pace to increase your heart rate, blood flow and circulation.

SOCIABLE. Whether it's a team-related sport or just something you do with someone else, exercise can be a great way of socializing and making friends, which in turn can improve your sense of well-being. A commitment to others makes it more likely to happen!

CHORES. It's amazing how much energy you can expend when vacuuming, dusting, cleaning, polishing or washing windows. You get to exercise and have a nice, clean and tidy home!

GARDENING. If you have a garden, mowing the grass or weeding will help you get some exercise and it gets you out in the fresh air too.

STAIRWAY. Modern buildings are full of elevators. If you take the stairs, you get some important exercise. Even if it's going down the stairs only, it's still exercise. Make a habit of it and you'll start to make this normal behavior.

CYCLING. How about peddling to work or school? Or try getting out into the hills for some mountain-biking. There are lots of road cycling clubs these days for people of all capabilities and ages.

SWIMMING. Whether your excuse is you don't like to get your hair wet, or you feel self-conscious about your body, once you're in, you're just like everyone else. Swimming pools often have slots dedicated to learning or training, so if you're not very good at it, you can learn. Even a gentle paddle up and down the pool helps to flex the limbs.

MAKE IT HAPPEN. Schedule exercise in your calendar as though it is an important meeting – actually, it really is!

66. ADDICTION MANAGEMENT

> "People who have never had an addiction
> don't understand how hard it can be."
> (Payne Stewart, Professional Golfer)

Addiction is a very complex issue with a wide range of impacting variables, triggers and sources, associated with myriad personality types, social circumstances, individual backgrounds and upbringings. But what seems universal is that an addiction is something that has a hold over the addict, which impacts their lives negatively in some way.

The ingrained nature of addictions does not make it impossible to resolve, but coping with and resolving addictions can require a multi-level approach, often benefitting from consultations with a medical doctor, therapist and addiction specialist.

DENIAL. This is always the first and often greatest hurdle: admitting that you have an addiction. Once you get past denial, you're in a better position to do something about it. The brain can be very clever at justifying addiction.

IDENTIFICATION. Untangle the issue by examining what exactly your addiction is. Often one core addiction is masked by other connected ones. It's unusual to suddenly become addicted without some underlying source experience.

THERAPY. Don't feel you've got to do this all on your own. It might be a long journey and having a therapist to guide you will make a huge difference. Group therapy might connect you with like-minded individuals.

SHARE. Seek out someone you trust, or who has recovered from a similar addiction, to support you, but be wary of those who might collude with you and your addiction. It might require you to change your circle of friends. Avoid isolating yourself; we all need to be social.

DISTRACTION. Make a change in how you think, feel or behave by choosing alternative thoughts, emotions and behaviors. Change your state of mind by going for a walk, reading a book, doing a crossword, watching a movie or listening to music. What music makes you feel good?

TIMING. There's always a reason why "now" is not the right time to address the addiction. This is part of denial and a reluctance to commit to your change.

LEARN. Understand "you" and your addiction. Become an expert in learning about it; speak to people, go to meetings, research it and write a journal.

AVOIDANCE. Know what situations trigger your addictions most and replace them with alternatives.

WITHDRAWAL. You may suffer differing degrees of withdrawal depending on the addiction. See these as your body's message that it's recovering. Withdrawal can be as much psychological as physical.

DE-STRESS. Understand what stresses you and manage this. Find new and different ways to relax.

HEALTH. Your body can do amazing things if you're fit and healthy. Exercise, eat well, sleep and rest will give you a powerful feel-good tonic. Try mindfulness strategies.

RELAPSE. Don't give yourself a hard time if you relapse. Pick yourself up and start again.

TRIGGERS. Know your triggers; even after you have conquered the addiction, you may find reminders or certain situations that will trigger a craving. Sometimes you can't avoid these triggers, but know in advance your game plan and then stick to it.

NEW LIFE. Don't see the end of an addiction as something you're giving up; rather, see it as part of the new life that you're creating and something great you're gaining.

Always check with your medical doctor before stopping addictions abruptly, especially with alcohol.

67. WEIGHT MANAGEMENT

"The unfortunate thing about this world is that good habits are so much easier to give up than bad ones."
(Somerset Maugham, Playwright and Novelist)

What we eat has a significant impact on our bodies. We're all naturally different shapes and sizes, and so what's sufficient nourishment for one may be different for another. But we can all potentially overeat and suffer the consequences of weight gain.

When more of us become overweight, it normalizes obesity. If everyone around us is overweight, and so are we, then we feel this is normal. But that doesn't make it healthy.

Conventional wisdom has suggested that being overweight can be reversed by dieting. But there's more to it than that – much of it has to do with our attitude to eating and adopting a healthy lifestyle.

REJOICE. Yes, that's the first thing to do when embarking on a healthy lifestyle. You're on the journey to feeling and looking terrific!
ROUTINE. Keep to a regular eating cycle, rather than skimping on meals. Eat a small amount regularly rather than large binge meals. It helps to burn calories faster.
COMPANY. Having a new way of eating or exercising more can feel

monotonous, but having someone to do it with, and feel accountable to, can really help get results.

BREAKFAST. It might seem tempting to quit breakfast, but this is an important meal, breaking the fasting from your night-time sleep. It'll stop the mid-morning snack temptation too.

LIQUID. Water is important to keep the body hydrated; drinking water regularly can also help when you're tempted to snack. Depending on your weight, you should be drinking over a litre of water each day.

SNACK ATTACK. Don't buy snacks. If you have them in the cupboard, you'll eat them. Period. They're rarely nutritious and are loaded with fat, sugar and salt. They're small but pack an unhealthy punch.

FRUIT 'N VEG. Eat five portions of fruit and vegetables each day. This can be any combination and in surprisingly smaller quantities that you'd think. Eating fruit as a snack can be really helpful.

HIGH FIBRE. This is found in plant foods, such as fruit and vegetables, beans, oatmeal, rice and pastas. These can also make you feel full, which helps reduce the amount you want to eat.

EXERCISE. Any form of exercise that increases the heart rate can be beneficial. (See Exercise)

SUGAR DRINKS. Fizzy carbonated drinks, some fruit drinks and alcoholic beverages have large amounts of sugar in them. Check the labels for sugar content and you'll be shocked.

PLAN. Lots of unhealthy eating comes from grabbing last-minute ready-to-eat meals. It's likely to be more expensive and loaded with sugar, salt and fat. Plan your meals at least a week in advance.

ROTATE. Plan different meals on different days for variety in your diet. Try one evening with fish or low-fat chicken or pork or pasta?

PLATE SIZE. The bigger the plates, the more you're likely to fill them.

ALCOHOL. According to www.drinkaware.co.uk, a glass of wine can have the same calories as four cookies or biscuits. A pint of beer can be equivalent to a slice of pizza! Say no more.

68. ACUTE AND CHRONIC PAIN

"Find a place inside where there's joy, and the joy will burn out the pain." (Joseph Campbell, Mythologist and Writer)

Acute pain is short term and covers issues like sprains, broken bones, labor and childbirth, dental work, etc. These injuries usually heal. By contrast, chronic pain lasts more than three months and is associated with severe headaches, lower-back pain, cancer, arthritis and nerve damage.

While other people might be able to see the physical effects of the pain, it's usually difficult to get a sense of its emotional and psychological affects. Pain is a message from the brain that something is wrong, but the brain can sometimes send conflicting signs and confuse what is wrong. Half the battle is working out the real cause and the other half is about living a full life, even with the pain.

ACUTE PAIN. If you experience an unusual pain, one that is excruciating or ongoing, get it checked out by your medical doctor or visit the emergency department.

NON-PRESCRIPTION. Don't under-estimate the benefits of non-prescription "wonder-drugs". People often think that only prescription medications are good. Wrong. Be careful, though, as even non-prescription medications can become addictive.

ACCEPTANCE. Appreciate that you will have good days and bad days. It's OK to have bad days, but know that you'll have good days again soon. It's about accepting the reality of the situation and not giving yourself a hard time emotionally.

AGEING. As part of the ageing process, you're going to notice things you can't do as well as you did in the past. That's normal. It happens to everyone.

LIMITATIONS. Find the point up to which you feel pain or find that it worsens. Ensure that you stop doing an activity before you reach this point. This becomes easier with practise and self-monitoring.

JOURNAL. Create a "pain diary" to monitor what contributes to good and bad days, and plan accordingly.

EXERCISE. Some exercise can help improve your posture, maintain muscle tone, increase your confidence, boost mood and general well-being, and reduce the fear of your pain. (See Exercise)

RELAX. While it's good to exercise, it's also good to relax and soothe your mind and body. This is about self-care, looking after yourself and appreciating your limits.

STAY POSITIVE. Guard against negative thinking, which can pull you down emotionally and lead to depressive thoughts and potentially reinforce the pain. (See Negative Thinking)

CLINICS. Some pain clinics offer a structured rehabilitation and normalization plan. Check with your medical doctor about what is available in your area.

LIMITATIONS. Advances in medicine give the impression that there's a cure for everything. Surgery doesn't always provide the solution and can make things worse.

INDIVIDUAL. It's your pain; you manage it your way. Medication isn't going to solve everything, though it may ease symptoms. It's about creating your personal plan, what you can do to think differently, act differently and behave differently to limit the impact pain has.

69. WORK-LIFE BALANCE

"Never get so busy making a living that you forget to make a life."
(Anon)

No one ever said on their death-bed, "I wish I'd spent more time at work". Yet, we spend an inordinate amount time working, earning a living, seeking that next promotion, competing with colleagues, pitching for that next contract and juggling competing demands. It's exhausting.

But it's important, too. Work gives us meaning, an identity, a sense of worth, an income, motivation, inspiration, drive, passion and meaning. There also needs to be a balance.

WORK SMART, NOT LONG. Give yourself a specific time for each task and limit activities that take up time, like pointless meetings about meetings.

PRIORITIZE. Plan what's important and schedule accordingly. Monitor the time spent on different tasks. (See Planning and Prioritizing)

FOCUS. Concentrate on one thing at a time. Juggling means you dilute your time and mind, and that takes more effort.

WHEEL OF LIFE. Draw a circle and write inside the segments of your life: partner, family, community, health, career, friends, relaxation and enjoyment ... and apportion time for each.

PERFECTIONISM. Let go and give yourself a break. No one's perfect.

ASSERTIVENESS. Sometimes it's hard to say "no". But there is a limit. Have the strength of your convictions and know when you have too much work or you need to delegate. (See Assertiveness)

EMAILS. We might regard social media as home-time territory, but many still clock into work emails. Don't. They can usually wait until the next working day. (See Email Etiquette)

STRESS. When work pressure exceeds your ability to cope, you feel stressed. Know the sources of stress for you and how to manage them better. (See Stress)

RELATIONSHIPS. Factor in allotted time for partners and family, whether it's evening or weekends.

TAKE A HOLIDAY. Lots of people don't take their full holiday entitlement, which means you're effectively working for free if you don't.

LIFESTYLE. Does your personal routine feed a poor work-life balance? Monitor what you drink and eat, the amount you exercise and the fresh air you get.

ADRENALINE. Beware of getting addicted to the cut and thrust of work. Pressure triggers an adrenalin rush, so factor in some down time to enable you to calm down.

EXERCISE. Build in regular exercise into your non-work routine. Team sports and activities help you to commit to others, so you will be less likely to shirk attendance!

BOUNDARIES. Sometimes say "no" and schedule time when you're "off radar" from work.

MINDFULNESS. If your brain's permanently active, learn to meditate, or take up yoga or Pilates. These help to calm and ground you.

"ME" TIME. Schedule in one thing to look forward to each day or factor in some private time.

HELP. If you feel stuck in a rut, ask for help. Speak to friends or work colleagues. Ask them what they do in similar situations. Perhaps see a therapist. (See Asking For Help)

70. THE FUTURE – BE YOUR OWN THERAPIST

*"We are made wise not by the recollection of our past,
but by the responsibility for our future."*
(George Bernard Shaw, Playwright)

We've written this book to empower you to make new choices about life issues. We hope that you'll start to see a pattern of guidance that helps you to ask questions about yourself and your situation. If you learn to listen to your body, mind and soul, then you are better able to find answers that are right for you.

In this final chapter, we leave you with several ways to help you become your own therapist. Not by talking to yourself in front of a mirror (although for some, it has been known to help!), but through systematically encouraging you to understand yourself more and to gain greater insights into your life. After all, you know yourself better than anyone!

SOLUTIONS. In Solution-Focused Therapy, this miracle question is used to find a way forward: if you woke up tomorrow and your problem was resolved, what would be different? Very simply put, you then work out what you'd be doing differently, knowing you have reached the solution. Then "what you are doing differently" is put into action (de Shazer, 1985).

PROBLEMS. Gerard Egan's model of the "skilled helper" suggests a problem-focused strategy: identify your problem, seek out blind spots and priorities, establish possibilities, an agenda and a commitment, then resolve with strategies, best fits and an action plan (Egan, 1994).

MENTOR. Who inspires you? This can be a historical figure or a sporting legend you admire. What would they say to you about your issue or how would they deal with it?

FUTURE YOU. On the basis that you know yourself best, if you were a wiser and older version of you, say 20 years from now, how would that "clever you" advise the you of today?

SEMANTICS. Spelling out your issue in as many ways as you can gives you different perspectives. Use different words to describe your problem.

YES, BUT. Therapists often pick away at things we say to help drill down to the heart of the matter. If you feel stressed, say, "Yes, but what's that about?" It might be frustration; "Yes, but what's that about?" "Well, it's feeling ignored", so go on to ask, "Yes, but what's that about?" "Well, I put the work in and didn't get credit" – and so on, until you get to the root issue. Once you're there, you have options for the required action.

EMPATHY. This is about understanding other people. By learning to be empathic, you'll understand others better and by doing so, you'll get to know yourself too. (See Empathy)

COMMUNICATION. What does communication mean to you? Getting your point across? It's an active, two-way process that requires give and take from both sides. I bet you know someone who speaks "at" you rather than "with" you. Annoying isn't it?

ACTIVE LISTENING. Do you really hear what other people are say-ing? It's not just the words, but the emotions behind them, the body language, the unspoken implicit messages and body cues. If no one is listening, then no one's being heard.

PERSONAL DEVELOPMENT. How do you develop as a person? Do you have a plan associated with how you'll grow, learn and develop as a human being?

EMOTIONAL INTELLIGENCE. EI is being intelligent about your emotions, but first you have to know what they are. Why do you express certain emotions at specific times? Are they appropriate? How else might you manage them? (See Emotional Intelligence)

PEOPLE SKILLS. Most managers are good at their jobs, but can be poor managers of others because they've never really been taught people skills or the "soft-skills" of empathy, communication and listening.

MINDFULNESS. A hectic, busy life makes it difficult to pause and take stock of things. Give yourself over to an activity that offers inner peace, like meditation, yoga or Pilates. Even a slow walk in the countryside listening to nature can allow you space to connect.

LOVE YOURSELF. You might love your partner, your kids, your football team – but do you love yourself? If not, why not? Ground yourself in self-value, self-worth and self-appreciation. Love the many unique qualities and characteristics of yourself. Ask for feedback from others about what they appreciate in you; you might be surprised.

HELP OTHERS. There's no better feel-good factor that when you know you've helped someone. Can you give a hand to someone who's less able than you, offer a listening ear, provide some tuition or guidance, connect with the elderly or the isolated, or offer your services in volunteering?

CONNECT. We're social creatures. We like to be with people, to share the ups and downs of life. How can you better connect with the people who are good for you and who enrich your life?

CHANGE. We might find change threatening at times, but sometimes it's the best solution. If you're in a dead-end job or relationship, maybe the best thing is to get out and make a change.

HAVE FUN. The elusive quest to be happy is often misconstrued because we all have a different concept of what constitutes happiness. But you know when you're having fun. And if you're having fun, it's likely you're happy. Go on, have some fun.

LEARN. Many of us stop wanting to learn because we had bad experiences at school. But having an enquiring mind, enjoying learning new things and stimulating our brains all help to develop and widen our perspective on life.

HEALTHY LIFESTYLE. You can't function on maximum capacity if you're not looking after your body. Exercise frequently, eat a balanced and nutritious diet, sleep and rest, derive the stimulation and motivation from work that's good for you, and last, but certainly not least, enjoy and nurture family and relationships.

The future's bright. The future's all yours.

Over to you ... we wish you well!

de Shazer, S. *Keys to Solution in Brief Therapy.* New York: Norton (1985). Egan G. *The Skilled Helper. A Problem-Management Approach to Helping.* CA: Brooks Cole Publishing (1994)

ABOUT THE AUTHORS

Rick Hughes

Rick has been a counsellor, coach, senior clinician, post-trauma consultant and employee support trouble-shooter for more than 20 years. He is Head of Service for Aberdeen University Counselling Service, before which he was Lead Advisor: Workplace for the British Association for Counselling and Psychotherapy. Rick worked in advertising and marketing before changing careers early into counselling and psychotherapy. He has a business degree, an MPhil in Emotional Intelligence, diplomas in Marketing and Counselling and an Honorary Research Fellowship from Strathclyde University.

Andrew Kinder

Andrew is a British Psychological Society Registered Coach and a chartered counselling and occupational psychologist. He was recognized by the British Association for Counselling and Psychotherapy with a Fellowship for his contribution to workplace counselling. He has published widely, particularly in the areas of work-related stress, trauma and stress management and is currently clinical director of a large employee assistance programme provider (EAP). He is active as a coaching practitioner with his own caseload of clients. www.andrewkinder.co.uk

Professor Sir Cary Cooper, CBE

Cary L. Cooper is the author and editor of more than 150 scholarly books and is one of Britain's most quoted business gurus. He is the 50th Anniversary Professor of Organizational Psychology and Health at Manchester Business School, University of Manchester. He is a founding President of the British Academy of Management, a Companion of the Chartered Management Institute and one of only a few UK Fellows of the (American) Academy of Management, President of the Chartered Institute of Personnel and Development (CIPD), President of RELATE, President of the British Academy of Management and President of the Institute of Welfare. He was the founding editor of the Journal of Organizational Behavior, former editor of the scholarly journal *Stress and Health* and is the editor-in-chief of the Wiley-Blackwell Encyclopaedia of Management, now in its third Edition. He was awarded the CBE by the Queen in 2001 for his contributions to occupational health and safety; and in 2014 he was awarded a Knighthood for his contribution to the social sciences.

ALSO BY THE SAME AUTHORS

Hughes R, Kinder A, Cooper C (Eds) *International Handbook of Workplace Trauma Support* Wiley-Blackwell. Chichester, UK (2012).

Kinder A, Hughes R, Cooper C (Eds) *Employee Well-Being Support – a Workplace Resource* Wiley-Blackwell, Chichester, UK (2008).

To contact the authors please email thecrisisbook@yahoo.com